The Sense of Significance

The Sense of Significance

THE

FRIENDSHIP

BETWEEN

CHRISTOPHER MORLEY

AND

BUCKMINSTER FULLER

———

Louise Morley Cochrane

First published in Great Britain in 2015
by Sidaway and Barry.

ISBN: 978-0-9931932-0-0

Designed and typeset by Mark Blackadder

Printed and bound in Britain by Bell and Bain Ltd, Glasgow

Contents

Preface

This is a limited edition book privately produced to commemorate the 125th birthday year of our grandfather, Christopher Morley (1890–1956), an American writer, journalist and broadcaster. It was written by his eldest daughter, our mother, Louise Morley Cochrane, who died in Edinburgh in February 2012.

She wrote it to record the deep friendship between Christopher Morley and the designer and inventor Richard Buckminster Fuller (1895–1983). Bucky summarised this in a letter to Louise in 1975: 'Mutual sense of significance continually re-inspired our friendship.' The book chronicles their early meetings, journeys together, subsequent contact, and the important influence each had on the other.

Louise wrote the book between 1975 and 1982 at Bucky's suggestion and with his active participation. It was based on her extensive interviews with him, which she recorded on tape, and her own research into correspondence and diaries. It was never published, but copies were sent to various interested people. In 2003 she gave copies of the final manuscript to the academic institutions with relevant collections. For Chris, these were the Harry Ransom Center (HRC) at the University of Texas in Austin, Texas, and Haverford College, Pennsylvania. For Bucky, this was the R. Buckminster Fuller Collection at Stanford University, California. Louise also donated the tapes of her interviews with Bucky, and a copy of the manuscript, to the British Library, so they are available for researchers. The British Library now holds the copyright of the tape-recordings.

We present this book as Louise wrote it, apart from an occasional emendation to clarify a point or a quotation. We have also added brief timelines for both Chris and Bucky for chronological context. We have not added explanations on areas which Louise thought self-explanatory. We think the book's importance is the insight it provides into a friendship of great significance to both men.

We would like to thank all those who have encouraged and helped us in this project, but are grateful above all to Allegra Fuller Snyder for her enthusiastic support.

Alison Barry and Janet Sidaway

Author's Note

This is a book about the friendship between two quite disparate personalities of the twentieth century, and the influence they had on each other in the course of their lives. One was the author Christopher Morley, the other was the inventor Buckminster Fuller. The book is based on correspondence between the two men and quotations from Christopher Morley's writings, as well as on interviews and correspondence between Buckminster Fuller and me.

The interviews took place before the discovery of the carbon molecule known as buckminsterfullerene. Nobel Prize winner Professor Sir Harold Kroto has said that he gave the name to the carbon molecule because it reminded him of the dome in Montreal which had been designed by Buckminster Fuller. He was taking his child in a pushchair around the interior of the dome when he suddenly appreciated the significance of the relationship between hexagons and pentagons.

The story of the step by step emergence of Bucky's design and Chris's supportive role emerges in the following pages.

The unpublished sources on which this book is based are as follows:

1 Christopher Morley Papers, including his personal diaries as well as correspondence with Buckminster Fuller, 1934–1955, held by the Harry Ransom Humanities Research Center, University of Texas at Austin, Texas,[1] and the

Bryant Library, Roslyn, Long Island, New York.

2 Letters and memorabilia received from Christopher Morley by Buckminster Fuller, 1934–1955, held in 'Chronofile', Stanford University.

3 Tape-recorded Interviews between Buckminster Fuller and Louise Cochrane:
>London, England, 23 September 1975.
>Philadelphia, PA, 5 November 1975.
>New York City, 17 November 1975.
>Philadelphia, PA, 22 November 1975.
>Wiltshire, England, 23, 24, 25 March 1976.
>Wiltshire, England, 29, 30 June 1976.

Louise Morley Cochrane

Editors' Note: British dates and spelling were used by Louise in the commentary and references, but when quoting from the correspondence and diary entries, she carefully reproduced exactly what Chris and Bucky wrote, including abbreviations, underlining and formatting.

Child and Universe:
The Time Dimension

In the New York City of the mid 1930s it would have been hard to find two more contrasting personalities than Christopher Morley and Buckminster Fuller; yet they became fast friends and remained such until Chris's death in 1957. At the time Chris was the popular figure – well known as the author of several highly successful books, founding editor of the *Saturday Review of Literature* and a judge of the Book-of-the-Month Club. In those pre-television days he was greatly in demand as a lecturer. He was ebullient, witty, effervescent. Even behind glasses his eyes were a sparkling and friendly blue. He was an expansive conversationalist and all who listened to him were his friends. It was otherwise when he shut himself away with his typewriter at home. He always worked under the pressure of deadlines. A hush descended lest he be disturbed.

Chris was not a tall man although he was generously built. It was more the warmth of his nature which seemed to give him pre-eminence in company. Bucky on the other hand was quite short. He seemed almost dwarfed by the large three-wheeled Dymaxion car which he had invented and which could turn on itself in the midst of city traffic to the amazement of passers-by. He too wore glasses and was very near-sighted. He peered from behind them with a look of intense concentration. At this time he was not the articulate speaker he became later. He was shy and diffident until he was confident that a listener was sympathetic to his ideas. Then he became effusively voluble but it was difficult to follow his train of thought.

I met Bucky first when I was fifteen. Christopher Morley was my father, and Bucky came frequently to our home. He was very interested in young people and would abandon the adults in a room to talk to you if you were prepared to listen. My first recollection of him is of his pointing out interesting aspects of the geometry exercise I was doing for homework. He got quite excited just talking about it.

Both Chris and Bucky had many other friends but this friendship was somehow different. For one thing it tran-scended the barriers supposed to exist between artist and scien-tist. Why were the men so attracted to each other's ideas?

As Chris had once said, 'It is confirmation that human beings most passionately seek . . . in order that ideas may move along their destined loops and altering orbits.' This mutual confirmation was what their friendship provided.

The surviving letters which they wrote to each other reveal little of what they discussed in person. Towards the end of his life Bucky filled in the background for me in a series of inter-views. He suggested that we meet and talk so that he could record what the friendship with Chris had meant to him. Our meetings took place between 1976 and 1981. A joint book was nearly complete when Bucky died. He had suggested as title *The Sense of Significance*, quoting from an essay which Chris had published in *The Romany Stain* in 1926:

> One can only fall back on the instinctive Sense of Significance, that subtle and massive intuition that must be (for every type of creator I suppose) the captain of his seven deadly senses. The Sense of Signifi-cance! Yes, that occult and instantaneous decision that certain gestures, certain random incidents, are neces-sary parts of the composition of our world. This instinct is capricious and quick, often one is puzzled to

know why such petty observations come full of meaning, magically confluent with the dark undercurrent of the mind.[1]

As Bucky remarked (letter to the author, 19 August 1976):

Here Chris was identifying the complex integral with which I am preoccupied and identify as Synergetics. Mutual sense of significance continually re-inspired our friendship.[2]

What Chris and Bucky understood by the sense of significance was the mystic and powerful intuition which helps the poet and the scientist to find meaning beyond the usual five senses and even beyond the unifying sixth or common sense. Bucky's contention was that, using this extra sense, Chris had observed in Nature the same principles which led him to the invention of the geodesic dome and synergetic geometry. For Chris the sense of significance provided the evocative imagery of his writing. It was as poet that Chris was interested in both nature and science. In *Inward Ho* (1923) he reflected:

Nature's whole complexion is one of entrancing appeal. And so, even though we only catch her sense at two removes, we all, scientists, philosophers, theologians, painters, poets, according to the measure of our individual hardihood pursue her in our own ways . . . How many thunderstorms circled the globe in gold and purple before man saw what she was driving at – offering us the subway, the telephone, the radio. What was it Walt Whitman said? 'I find letters from God dropt in the street'.[3]

Before they met, both men had enjoyed actively exploring ideas of self and universe. Both had an acute awareness of

Cosmos and recognised that a revolution had taken place in man's concept of reality in their own lifetime. Bucky wondered whether evolution in the universe was following a mathematical pattern which man could understand and conceptualise. Chris was more concerned with self-identification, the effect of the dramatically changed world on human spirit and intellectual freedom.

The friendship between the two men had its roots some years before they met in person. Bucky had been very touched by a poem which Chris had written in 1920.

TO A CHILD

The greatest poem ever known
Is one all poets have outgrown
The poetry, innate, untold
Of being only four years old.

Still young enough to be a part
Of Nature's great impulsive heart,
Born comrade of bird, beast and tree
And unselfconscious as the bee –

And yet with lovely reason skilled
Each day new paradise to build,
Elate explorer of each sense
Without dismay, without pretense!

In your unstained, transparent eyes,
There is no conscience, no surprise:
Life's queer conundrums you accept,
Your strange divinity still kept.

Being that now absorbs you all
Harmonious, unit, integral,
Will shred into perplexing bits, –
Oh, contradictions of the wits!

And life, that sets all things in rhyme,
May make you poet, too, in time –
But there were days, O tender elf,
When you were Poetry itself.[4]

In Bucky's view the publication of this poem was the start of the friendship. At our first interview Bucky recited the poem from beginning to end. He still knew it by heart. Bucky explained:

There is no question but that the poem brought us together. I read it in the 'Bowling Green', Chris's old *New York Evening Post* column, a few days before our daughter Alexandra died. She was four years old. I memorised it and when I met your father twelve years later I recited it. Chris was very deeply moved. 'I'd really forgotten I'd written that poem, but I remember it now' was what he said.[5]

It would have always been easy for people to nod sympathetically when Bucky recited the poem, which apparently he did often, and then dismiss its importance as being purely sentimental. How natural for bereaved parents to find comfort in the simple charm of another father's delight in his child. But the poem meant more than that.

The sense of universe in the child has been variously described. It is inherent in Wordsworth's poem 'We Are Seven', as De Quincey pointed out, and also in his 'Ode: Intimations of Immortality'. It is Koestler's oceanic sense. For Bucky the companion poem to Chris's is Kipling's 'Merrow Down'.

Kipling also had a daughter who died tragically young.

Bucky felt that he was led intuitively to his original ideas about the basic structure of the universe by contemplating the mystic relationship between child and Nature. The importance of Chris's poem in their subsequent friendship must not be underestimated as it started Bucky off on his train of thought which led ultimately to the geodesic dome:

> Later, in my book *Nine Chains to the Moon*, which your father was responsible for getting published, I used the phrase 'your strange divinity still kept' about Alexandra and about our second daughter Allegra in my dedication. In 1962 I quoted that poem in my piece called 'Prospects for Humanity' in the fortieth anniversary number of the *Saturday Review of Literature*, which your father helped to found.[6]

It was not merely this poem but also Chris's book called *I Know a Secret* (1927) which appealed to Bucky. This was published when Allegra Fuller was a baby, and when Bucky faced an acute personal crisis. It was at this time that Bucky determined to take time out to think through the ideas which had been accumulating in his mind about 'man's relationship to the universe and the exploitation of Nature's laws to improve man's condition'. He set out then to develop what he later called his anticipatory design science and to record in his 'Chronofile' the events in his life to test whether mathematical laws applied to man's potential control over his environment.

As Bucky's ideas became clearer he wrote a book which he then mimeographed and bound. Two hundred copies were published in this form. The book was called 4D, meaning Fourth Dimension, a concept then widely being discussed in relation to Einstein's theories. In 1928 Bucky sent a copy of his 'Mimeograph Art' to Chris thinking he would be interested, an intuition he based on having read *I Know a Secret*

6

which he quoted in the text. The two men had not met. The accompanying letter was the first in their correspondence:

> *May 21, 1928*
>
> The greatest poem ever known which you wrote 'To a Child' has always been with me since our little daughter Alexandra died six years ago, a few days before her fourth birthday. Allegra was born last August and is just what her name implies. A close feeling of kinship for you, derived from reading such harmonious and essential thoughts as are written into *I Know a Secret* allows my asking that you read this paper.[7]

Although Chris did not appear ever to have answered the letter, a copy of *4D* turned up later among his papers. What were the 'harmonious and essential thoughts' which prompted Bucky to write as he did?

Bucky told me that Chris has explained the title himself when he described one of the children. Bucky found the passage and read it aloud:

> Eyes roguish, her small positive person swinging gaily, definitely in time to the tune she was singing. 'I know a secret – I won't tell; I know a secret – I won't tell', she chanted. Yes, she knows a secret. What is it, I wonder? If *we* knew, you and I, it wouldn't be a secret. Sometimes I think I have guessed a hint of it, that the age between four and five is the most beautiful of all . . . she knows a secret, perhaps once we knew it too.[8]

And Bucky recalled:

> When I started my life all over again in 1927, determined to do my own thinking and wrote *4D*, I set out hopefully to recover all those childish sensitivities, intu-

itions and initiatives I'd had, and this effort was very much tied in with Chris's book *I Know a Secret*. That's why this book hit me so hard at that time. I felt Chris has never lost the sensitivity he'd had as a child or had already rediscovered what I was looking for. I was trying to regain this extraordinary thing we're born with. I'm writing now of the child as the absolutely pure scientist who bases his work only upon experimentally redemonstrated findings. One can see the child's sensitivity and the child's explanations are pure. They simply have to put their hands on everything and really check by experimental evidence. Chris understood about that.[9]

That Chris had indeed retained his early sensitivity, and cultivated it, was apparent in his writing. He had had an extremely happy childhood, first on the campus at Haverford College where his father was Professor of Mathematics and then in Baltimore where they moved when he was ten years old and his father became Head of the Post Graduate Department of Mathematics at Johns Hopkins University. After graduating from Haverford College, Chris revelled in his years at New College, Oxford, where he was a Rhodes Scholar. On his return to the United States he persuaded Frank Doubleday to give him a job in his famous publishing firm and in 1914 he married Helen Fairchild for whom he had written most of his early poems.

By 1922 there were three children: Chris Jr, Louise and Helen. Blythe was born the following year. Chris was already well enough established to support his family as a writer. *Parnassus on Wheels* (1917) and *The Haunted Bookshop* (1919) had been successful novels. *Chimneysmoke* (1921) was a popular book of early poems, and *Inward Ho* (1923) was a republication of essays which had appeared originally in newspaper columns. In 1922 Chris helped to found the *Saturday*

Review of Literature. Where the Blue Begins (1922), his satirical novel about contemporary society and man's search for a non-anthropomorphic God, was followed by *Thunder on the Left* (1925), a novel which explored in depth the theme of 'To a Child'. It was sufficiently powerful to prompt Kipling to seek his acquaintance, a most unusual move on Kipling's part. In 1927 Chris became a founding judge of The Book-of-the-Month Club, the same year that *I Know a Secret* was published.

In his career up to this time Bucky had faced many more problems than Chris had done. He had lost his father when he was twelve years old. He had left Harvard without graduating. Then in 1917 he joined the US Navy and a short course led to a commission. In July of that year he married Anne Hewlett.

He subsequently served on the USS *George Washington*, which carried President Wilson to the Versailles Conference. The ship was equipped with the latest in radio and telecommunication devices and Bucky was able to learn a great deal about them. He seemed well launched on a naval career. Then Admiral Gleave, for whom he was acting as aide, was transferred to command the Pacific fleet. Bucky was transferred with him. His daughter Alexandra, however, was stricken with polio and meningitis. Bucky felt he could not leave his wife and child in such circumstances. He was allowed to resign his commission.

After Alexandra's death in 1922, Bucky joined his father-in-law in business. This was not a success, and led to the period of crisis in which *4D* was written. Although Bucky spoke of a 'secret inspiration' derived from Chris's writing, his concept of the further dimension was the result of his own thinking. Having worked for five years in the building industry he was convinced that structural design in the future should make more sense of natural forces.[10]

One important aspect of Bucky's design was that it provided a visual concept of the further dimension equivalent

9

to a mental image of length, width and height. The structure for a house which Bucky outlined in 4*D* would be built around a central mast, implanted like the trunk of a tree. His fourth dimension was the radial distance outward horizontally from the mast. The horizontal radius would be expressed in units of time. What Bucky called 'time' in 4*D* he later called frequency. In 4*D* he was applying spherical trigonometry to building design.

Chris knew enough mathematics to grasp Bucky's ideas when they eventually met. He encouraged Bucky to persist with his challenge to those who thought it inconceivable to abandon the perpendiculars of the cubic building tradition. Chris himself had made a special study of spherical trigonometry to enable his canine hero, Mr Gissing, to plot a spiritual course. Mr Gissing was named after first of the Morley dogs, so-called because Chris was reading George Gissing the night the stray mongrel entered our lives. All the characters in *Where the Blue Begins* were dogs with human attributes. Space and time were important elements in the fantasy world which Chris created. Chris's imagery relating to the time dimension, however, always conveyed flowing movement. He did not visualise time as a static structure.

In *Thunder on the Left,* he wrote:

The broad stream of sunlight flowed through the house like a steady ripple of Lethe, washing away the sandy shelves of trivial Now, dissolving little edges of past and future into its current, drawing all Time together in one clear onward sluice . . .

. . . The day was going back to the pure darkness where all things began; to the nothing from which it had come; to the unconsciousness that had surrounded it. The long, long day had orbed itself to a whole. Its plot and scheme were perfect; its crises and suspenses artfully ordered; now darkness framed it and memory gave it grace. Tented over by upward and downward light, mocked by tinsel colors and impossible desires, another cunning microcosm was complete.

Chris saw time as having a dream quality of movement in eternity. He spoke of children again in relation to this.

> People pretend that children are just human beings of a smaller size, but I think they're something quite different. They live in a world with only three dimensions, a physical world immersed in the moment, a reasonable world, a world without that awful sorcery of a fourth measurement that makes us ill at ease. What is it their world lacks? Is it self-consciousness, is it beauty, is it sex? (Three names of the same thing, perhaps.)[11]

In *Thunder on the Left*, Chris enabled a boy of ten, Martin, to project himself in time and spy on the adult world in which the hero, George, was himself grown up. Martin retained as adult all the honesty and simplicity of a child and caused havoc at a weekend house party in which he became involved. He was then horrified to realise that George was the man he would become.

Chris had now achieved a leading position among writers of his generation. His work continued to reveal his interest in the prevailing currents of scientific thought. In *Human Being* (1933) he wrote:

> Which is more important, to split the Atom or to split the idea? Why be so startled at the thought that Space is curved? Thought too is curved, returns upon itself, occupies many spaces at once. Is the atom a little solar system? So is each idea a microcosm of its thinker's identity. The noble human mind in whose sight eternity is but a day.[12]

For Bucky, reflecting retrospectively, this statement was extremely important:

> The comment about the atom is really profound. What Chris says here is what I've been saying about the tetrahedron as the minimal structural system of the universe. It is both the physical and metaphysical quantum unit. It is minimally defined by four points – to my mind the way all thought occurs. Ideas are systemic and formed this way . . . When you say 'I understand' you mean you have interlinked all the points in the system so they interconnect most economically.[13]

Bucky had not thought before his meeting with Chris that his pattern of universe might be related to patterns of thought or shapes of ideas. This came later. Bucky was convinced, however, that as a child he had recognised intuitively a principle of nature which it was important to utilise to man's advantage. The recent discovery of a carbon molecule whose atoms assume the basic shapes Bucky used in the design of a geodesic dome has confirmed his theory. The molecule has been called buckminsterfullerene in his honour. The inherent symmetry of the tetrahedron's dimensions is that of the 'golden section'. This might account for the stability and the versatility which Bucky exploited.

After publication of 4D he constructed a model of his house which would use highest performance materials of the type employed in aircraft. Make the most with the least, that was the principle and meaning of the word 'Dymaxion'. The term was invented by advertising men from Marshall Field, the big Chicago department store. They copyrighted it in Bucky's name because they wanted to use his model house to promote a line of modern furniture. Marshall Field staff thought the term 4D was too liable to misinterpretation. The furniture sold well but the house as designed then was never built.

Bucky now applied his ideas to the manufacture of a Dymaxion car on his completely new design principle. The tubular framework was a tetrahedron. There was great interest in the car. Unfortunately a bad accident destroyed the first one in 1933. It was rammed by another car in a collision en route to the airport following successful tests on behalf of a group of English automobile enthusiasts. The driver of the Dymaxion was killed and his English passenger very badly injured. By the time the police arrived the other car had been removed. Subsequent bad publicity meant the withdrawal of sponsorship even though the coroner's inquest exonerated the Dymaxion car. Bucky risked all his financial resources to continue production with a second and then a third.

In the spring of 1934 when the second Dymaxion car was the talk of the town in New York, Chris and Bucky met face to face for the first time. Chris was forty-four and Bucky was thirty-nine. Chris had written in February 1934, perhaps presciently:

> Every living creature, I read in the newspaper, has its own special wave-length, which, if tuned in upon may produce extraordinary results. Perhaps 1934 was going to be somewhere closer to our own frequency.[14]

Dymaxion Heyday

When the Depression of the 1930s seriously affected Chris's finances he closed up the house in Roslyn, Long Island, and moved the family temporarily into New York City. By 1934 the city's despair was receding. We looked down from an apartment on Riverside Drive and could see the smoking campfires of the shanty town built by the unemployed across the railroad tracks, but Franklin Roosevelt's New Deal was beginning to have a real impact. The city was emerging from the bitter years. The Empire State Building altered the skyline. There were still trolley cars on Broadway and milk was delivered from horse drawn carts but the new bridges and parkways under construction pointed towards the future. Rockefeller Center and Radio City were a mecca for tourists and New Yorkers alike.

Bucky had also moved from Chicago to New York by this time and was receiving a good deal of favourable publicity for the second Dymaxion car. Its unusual appearance was capable of stopping traffic and Bucky enjoyed showing off its manoeuvrability, especially with journalists in the car. As it happened, Frank Morley, Chris's brother, arranged to introduce Bucky to Chris. Frank was a director of the publishing firm of Faber and Faber in London and had come to do some business in New York. He had become acquainted with Bucky through English engineering friends. Bucky remembered:

Thanks to Frank, Chris asked me to come to the Three Hours for Lunch Club. We became great friends right away. There was something very powerful and intuitive about our feeling for each other. We were both not only willing to listen to one another, we listened enthusiastically. I was really entranced by the way Chris thought, spoke and wrote and he felt about me the same way. This was quite different from being tolerant of one another, listening to one another's papers, giving and accrediting but no sympathy. In some way we were tuned to one another.[1]

The Three Hours for Lunch Club was a purely ad hoc group. Prohibition had been repealed and people could have an alcoholic drink in a bar or restaurant without feeling guilty. Chris and his friends met often and occasionally indulged in very prolonged lunches at a restaurant (formerly a 'speakeasy') run by Chris Cella. They called these sessions the Three Hours for Lunch Club. Meetings were arranged by Chris, usually when he sought diversion between bouts of concentrated literary output. Among the 'regulars' were Don Marquis, Bill Benet, Bill Hall, Simeon Strunsky, Franklin Adams, and Clifton Fadiman. The sessions were fairly bibulous. One major criterion was that all participants would enjoy themselves in an uninhibited way and Bucky was very happy to join in. Soon he and Chris were meeting even more frequently.

On 31 March 1934, Chris devoted his *Saturday Review* column, 'The Bowling Green', to his 'Thoughts in a Dymaxion Car' under the main title *Streamlines*. Chris used the car as a symbol and jumping off point for social comment:

I'm interested in this not just as a car,
Which is relatively unimportant,
But as a symbol of what is forward
In every phase of living.

Not only in locomotion, architecture, shipbuilding,
but in morals and manners, clothes, religions,
 even in literature.
We grope for the Streamline: to reduce unnecessary
 wind resistance.

Chris derived enormous pleasure from his subsequent rides in the Dymaxion. A year later in his column:

I have spoken here before of Mr Buckminster Fuller's Dymaxion car, a completely streamlined automobile which has three wheels, steers from the tail and looks very like a huge fish. One of the noticeable features of a ride in a fully streamlined car is that even at high speed there is not the roaring fizz of air when another car is met. The streamline shape cuts down the atmospheric torture; it swims cleanly through the air without creating turbulence of the spinning eddies to impact upon the air broken by another car. And this, too, if one cared to pursue the thought has analogies in the realm of thinking, even in theology and politics.[2]

In the summer of 1934 Chris travelled to South America on board the SS *Santa Maria* of the Grace Line. He went as the guest of the company to gather material for his column. Afterwards he wrote a travel book entitled *Hasta La Vista, A Postcard from Peru*. It was published the following spring (1935) and launched on its day of publication during a journey in the Dymaxion car. Bucky was driving Chris to a lecture engagement in Lowell and Chris told reporters in Boston that he had made the presentation to Bucky at midnight – 'the first time on record that a new book was publicly introduced in this way'.

Chris's first letter to Bucky, preserved in Bucky's 'Chronofile', again concerned the car:

June 8, 1936

I want a really fine photo of Dymaxion for a book I'm going to publish.

Bucky replied not only with a photograph but some material of his own on the subject. Towards the end of the summer Chris wrote again:

September 25, 1936

Magnificent Bucky:

There will be a book called *STREAMLINES* coming about November first in which you will find your name mentioned with affection and respect. It will contain a photograph of Lord Dymaxion and his Machine.

Now look here – I have got two or three or four lecture dates in New England on October 27, 28, 29 and perhaps 30th. They include Worcester, Mass and Middletown, Conn, and perhaps one or two female seminaries in that region. I was just wondering . . . anyhow give me ring at your convenience and let's confidentially discuss.

Yours for more and better coordinates and plotting paper.

Chris.[3]

Bucky replied:

Great Christopher,

Yrs re seminaries r'c'd. Definitely interested. Back N.Y.C. next week.

Yrs. Buckminster[4]

Rereading these letters reminded Bucky that in the early days of their friendship he had started to travel regularly with Chris on his lecture tours and they used the Dymaxion car. This was a great boon to Chris, who hated driving in traffic. Bucky and his family lived in Connecticut while work continued on the Dymaxion car – a good starting point for New England trips. The habit of travelling together continued when Bucky abandoned the Dymaxion for a more conventional vehicle. Chris had put forward a number of promotional ideas for Bucky's car but it was never mass produced. Bucky claimed, however, that he had not really thought of the car as a commercial undertaking:

> Looking back on this time quite a lot of people have said to me, 'What a pity the car wasn't a commercial success'. It is important to know that I did not develop the Dymaxion car for commercial reasons. I had no intention of becoming a car-producing business man.
>
> I had produced my car to try out principles which might one day be of advantage to humanity and I did not want humanity to put these to one side because the principles I employed had seemingly produced negative results. My mother died about the time of the Dymaxion car crash and I inherited a bit of money. I put it all into producing a second and a third car. Then I ran out of money and I closed up the works. At this time I began writing *Nine Chains to the Moon*. My friend Bill Osborn was director of research at Phelps Dodge, the third largest copper company in the world. In 1936 he opened their pure research department in contrast to their routine metallurgical analysis laboratories. He asked me to be his assistant and I accepted.[5]

During this time Chris and Bucky were seeing each other very regularly. Their ideas interacted, but above all they had fun. Chris had a character who appeared occasionally in his columns, called the Old Mandarin. He was very fond of mathematical games so Bucky taught the Old Mandarin numerology:

That was why the number 22 was so important in our relationship. 22 is the top number in numerology, 2 times 11. After I taught him numerology Chris had great fun with it. Allegra Fuller turned out to be a number 22. He wanted people to change their names after that to get 22.[6]

At the back of one of Chris's diaries he has the alphabet listed with a numerical equivalent of each letter to show how numerologists make their calculations:[7]

A = 1	N = 5		
B = 2	O = 6		
C = 3	P = 7		
D = 4	Q = 8	ALLEGRA	
E = 5	R = 9	1335791	1+3+3+5+7+9+1 = 29
			2+9 = 11
F = 6	S = 10	FULLER	
G = 7	T = 2	633359	6+3+3+3+5+9 = 29
			2+9 = 11
H = 8	U = 3		
I = 9	V = 4		
J = 10 = 1	W = 5	You add each group of digits together	11+11 = 22
K = 11 = 2	X = 6		
L = 3	Y = 7		
M = 4	Z = 8		

After Bucky had introduced Chris to numerology the two men continued to enjoy the discovery of 22 numbers for the rest of their lives. The twenty-second of the month took on a special meaning. It was a 22 day when *Hasta la Vista* was published and launched in the Dymaxion car. When Bucky was thinking of a name for a new company Chris spent some time working out the numerology of the various suggestions.

Neither of them ascribed supernatural powers to numerical relationships based on the alphabet as some people do. But Chris found the discussions useful when he wrote *The Trojan Horse* (1937). Cassandra utilised numerology to predict the tragedy of Troy. The letters of her name added up to 8 which had all the wrong vibrations. The favourable digits were all on the Greeks' side.

Although Chris used this type of material as copy he did not take it too seriously. In another column:

> As a mystic poor old 'Q' is only so so, believing that too deliberate or reckoned occultism is the gardenias, yet he confesses innocent happiness in all sorts of private totem and taboo. When for instance he found the number of the car was 1696, which adds up to 22, the numerologist's bliss, and the car next to it was 2216, the 'Electrical Eleven'.[8]

Chris had a number of literary characters who were projections of himself. 'Q' was P.E.G. Quercus. The Old Mandarin was one of his favourites and became more so during the years of close association with Bucky. It was at this time that many of Chris's friends and his family began to call him OM or 'Old Man', an affectionate shortening of Old Mandarin.

One of the earliest *Translations from the Chinese* for which the Old Mandarin was responsible had been written in 1922. Bucky copied the poem and kept it in one of his books:

> *How is it, by what incalculable instinct,*
> *That now and then, in a clean afternoon*
> *By some touch of air or slope of twilight,*
> *Without previous thought I say to myself*
>   *(And am unerringly right)*
> *It feels as if*
> *There were a new moon.*[8]

Bucky continued all his life to remark on this sensation:

> In addition to the calendar's 22 days we used to say
> 'Happy New Moon Day'. We both had that new moon
> feeling. We knew when there was going to be a new
> moon. We felt the feeling had to do with a gravitational
> and electromagnetic circuitry pull that made us feel the
> new moon was there.

Before they met, Chris, like Bucky, had a strong cosmic
sense, that of living on a planet like a ship revolving in space
and moving round the sun. He had described the feeling in
Where the Blue Begins (1922):

> The dogwood tree was now in flower. The blossoms
> with their four curved petals seemed to spin like white
> propellers in the bright air. When he saw them flutter-
> ing Gissing had a happy sensation of movement. The
> business of those tremulous petals seemed to be thrust-
> ing his whole world forward and forward through the
> viewless ocean of space. He felt as though he were on
> a ship – as indeed we are.[10]

Bucky later popularised the concept of 'Spaceship Earth':

> I used the phrase for the first time in 1951 when the
> rocket program was just beginning. I was answering a
> question at the end of a lecture to a large audience at
> the University of Michigan. A student asked me what
> it was like to be on a spaceship and I said, 'What does
> it feel like to you right now? You've never known
> anything else. We live on Spaceship Earth, making
> 67,000 miles per hour around the sun without any
> noise or tremor.'[11]

Chris often remarked on his feeling that mornings were upward slopes to the meridian and then downward slopes to evening. The friendship with Bucky strengthened both men's powers of observation. In 1936 Chris wrote an essay called *Principality and Power*, which became a special presentation book for the approaching World's Fair. In it he spoke of New York:

> Then suddenly I am lifted far above books into the unwritten and the unwritable. For the morning sun is just at the moment glazing crystal fire on the edge of the Empire State Building. 'Euclidean paradise of solids veined with parallels of silver' my friend Mistletoe once called it. Just at that ten o'clock moment the rising light is exactly at an oblique which catches the great perpendicular on tangent. The dazzle seems to bulge the rigid vertical into a burning curve, clear out of plumb. A suggestion for dogmatists I say to myself. The rising light of the future may show many of our right angled ideas on a new slope. Such is the vision of the Fair, a new kind of poetry if you like. New York has always been too subtle for word fanciers. The architects and engineers have been her poets. Their rhymes have been upended into space.[12]

A new slope for right angled ideas was what Bucky was considering at this time in an effort to conceptualise radiation. Chris had seen a dazzle of sunlight and perhaps thanks to conversations with Bucky he noticed something which he had not mentioned when he wrote about the same scene in *John Mistletoe* (1931), five years earlier. Bucky reflected:

> In his World's Fair passage Chris was intuiting the idea I've often thought about. In the universe as I see it there is no timeless height, width and breadth. There is only

22

convergence, divergence and comprehensive embrace-
ment. There is only radial in, out and around and their
radial or circumferential cyclic periodicities. This is the
time element I later called frequency. The 'new slope'
Chris spoke of would be my angle of radial divergence.

The fact that your grandfather was a mathematician was really very important to me because your
father encouraged me regarding the significance of my
energetic-synergetic geometry when there wasn't
anyone else around who understood. Chris couldn't
understand why the academic system wouldn't pay any
attention to me and my rationally volumed hierarchy
of regular polyhedral, you know, the Platonic solids, in
which I show that when the vector-edged tetrahedron
has the volume 1, the vector diagonalled cube has a
volume of exactly 3, the octahedron 4, the vector diam-
eter sphere 5, the rhombic dodecahedron 6 and the
vector equilibrium simultaneously +2½ and −2½.
Nobody in world history had discovered or realised
that this was mathematically demonstrable. This is
what Kepler was looking intuitively for when he made
his concentric symmetrical geometry model which he
sensed had some relationship to the solar system's
planets. This constant cosmic hierarchy is what I'll be
known for later if I'm known for anything at all. I
might as well say it here as Chris was so interested in
it and prone to think it had the critical significance for
humanity which I assumed it to have.[13]

I asked Bucky if he had worked out the details of the Vector
Equilibrium at this time and he said 'No' but he had been
thinking about it. I then remembered that my grandfather's
name [Frank Morley] is associated with a theorem about equilateral triangles. It establishes that the trisectors which lie adjacent to the sides of any triangle will always intersect to form

an equilateral triangle. Bucky at once stated that this was 'akin to his tetrahedronal coordinate system'. In due course he sent me a diagram and a detailed explanation. These are not easy for the uninitiated to understand. Bucky always insisted that he was led by intuition to feel that the tetrahedron had more potential for the exploitation of natural forces than the cube. In building structure he was thinking about the weight of the materials; in designing the Dymaxion car he was thinking about wind resistance. It was really not until he worked on the relationship between the radii of spheres and the chords of intersecting great circles or geodesics that the structural possibilities of the dome began to assert themselves. Bucky and Chris did not apparently discuss this theorem. The coincidence involved, however, would have appealed to them.

> Chris always said how interested his father would be in my geometry but it was he who was sympathetic to my ideas and participated in every way. He encouraged me to pursue intuitive formulations. He was older than I and it was the first intimate friendship I'd had with a scholar. I had all kinds of nice friends, many engineers, but Chris was a scholar and a poet.

I asked Bucky how much higher mathematics he thought my father understood. He replied:

> I think the problem intrigued him but he couldn't have written a full explanation in the way your grandfather or your uncle Frank Morley could. He was more interested in attitudes than in formal structure. But he knew enough to recognise the integrity of the theories we discussed; he didn't want to be a scientist. This conversation might give you the wrong impression about the times we had together, Chris was so extraordinary and the richness of his outpourings was such that I imagine

24

he spoke about a hundred words to my one. Most of the time I sat enraptured. He was a living poet. He talked as a poet. It kept coming out one flash after another. Some things I may have inspired him about but he was mostly self-inspiring.[14]

3

Streamlines

The dedication in 1936 of Chris's collection of essays entitled *Streamlines* was

> For BUCKMINSTER FULLER, scientific idealist . . .
> ['Whose innovations proceed not just from technical
> dexterity but from an organic vision of life.']¹

It showed how deeply Chris felt about Bucky. The two men shared intellectual perceptions of natural laws and an interest in contemporary streamline designs but their creativity was stimulated in quite different ways. Bucky was devising structures; Chris was more concerned with ideas. In his book, *Inward Ho!*, there are passages about poetry and science:

> Poetry deals with essences that are perpetually in motion: at the very start the poet verifies the dream of medieval science. The mind is the true *primum mobile* . . . Walt's [Whitman] obeisance to science . . . was usually a trifle humorous, but it was genuine. Walt was shrewd enough to perceive that poetry is really an extension or excurrency of the scientific spirit . . . The scientist is happy, I dare say, because he does sometimes succeed . . . He discovers some formula absolutely valid in itself, composes some machine that he can see working . . . But the poet never succeeds.²

In *The Romany Stain* Chris spoke of Havelock Ellis's *The Dance of Life* (published in 1923) particularly in relation to the essential unity of science and art, and wrote:

> These passages are the richest delight to anyone who has been privileged to guess the imaginative poetical spirit that irradiates all genuine scientific enquiry.[3]

Chris felt that literature provided the reader with opportunities to find out for himself what he required for spiritual enlightenment as well as for understanding the universe. He liked to discover what he felt others had discovered before him. The reader must collaborate with the author. In *John Mistletoe* he compared Prospero in *The Tempest* to a modern scientist:

> The island is the solitude of the mind, and Prospero represents Thought, Imaginative Creation of any sort. I like to think of him as a scientist of the Einstein, Jeans or Eddington type . . . like Professor Jeans' universe he was melting into radiation and knew it . . . when Prospero says the famous lines
>
> > *These our actors,*
> > *As I foretold you, were all spirits and*
> > *Are melted into air, into thin air . . .*
> > *This insubstantial pageant . . . We are such stuff*
> > *As dreams are made on, and our little life*
> > *Is rounded with a sleep,*
>
> he is in the very accent of the intuitive mathematicians who had dissolved all our old rule-of-thumb universe by the transition from Euclidean to non-Euclidean geometry.[4]

Chris had noticed the delicate balance of the forces in a spider's web and used this image to describe some of his own tensions:

I suppose it is valuable, for intellectual reasons, that a man's life should be as much of a paradox as possible. It has always amused me to observe that though all my best instincts are for lethargy, quietism, postponement and concentration, I usually find myself in a hurry. What an accurate word is *distracted,* for if I pause to examine my mind I can usually find it subject to various diverse tensions. Perhaps that is well: like the outer ligatures of a spider's web these help to keep the central gossamers of the spirit from collapsing into a silky tangle. And though theoretically I abhor the business of being in a hurry, yet I must be honest enough to confess that often it is in that condition that I find myself happiest. And how, otherwise, would the occasional interludes of exquisite indolence be so perfect? Evidently there is some deep necessity for life to be as full of opposites as possible.[5]

A line in a letter from Keats to Reynolds had always intrigued Chris: 'Now it appears to me that almost any man may, like the spider, spin from his own innards his own airy citadel'.[6]

Chris used this quotation on the title page of *Inward Ho!* He derived both pleasure and pain from his own self-analysis. He used himself as a prototype for many of his invented characters. He saw in the rapidly accelerating technological revolution the danger that man would release energy potential which the primitive social organisation of human relationships could not control. He was worried about the effect this would have on the human spirit. Only when self-analysis prevailed could people make a realistic use of the power at their disposal. The role of the writer was to reveal people to themselves, that of the inventor to help man improve his condition. Bucky, as inventor, was optimistic:

A number of writers were apprehensive about the new

technology. I had the responsibility of knowing that the universe is nothing but technology. Man in his ignorance and fear was using technology primarily for weapons and then much later realising that all his weapon-technology can be 'turned into plough shares'.

I'd seen the technology which came out of World War I and I wanted it to be used to give people better houses and better transport. I saw that the heart of technology is its mathematical coordination and that the universe is operating four dimensionally, not three dimensionally. That's what *4D* was all about.[7]

Chris had been writing about streamlining before he met Bucky and then used the Dymaxion car as a visible symbol of the relationship he had been exploring between scientific theory and natural fact as well as the impact of technology on literature.

The principal essay in the book was one entitled 'Streamlines (Thoughts in a Dymaxion Car)'. Chris expressed concern that civilisation should recognise the need to shed unnecessary wind resistances, the accretions which came with technology-distorted values. Advertising men were making people too concerned about personal fastidiousness. Judging from subway advertising, he thought that a visiting foreigner would assume that America's main concerns were 'thinning hair, fluent [sic] nose . . . tussive throat . . .'; but Dan Chaucer and Will Shakespeare took a little dandruff in their stride.[8]

He also remarked on imitative architecture:

Give me something to imitate cried the American
  architect,
planning Gothic cloisters and bell-towers for
  New England colleges.
Give me something to imitate and I'll make you the
  damndest biggest
finest most original imitation in the world.[9]

One of Chris's preoccupations at this time was with 'grotes-
quely accelerated behaviour'. In an essay entitled 'Epistle to
the Colossians' he remarked that letters dropped in the mail
chutes of the then new Empire State building fell so fast that
they had to be slowed down at the 65th and 38th floors to
prevent scorching. He then continued:

> Surely we need occasional slow-down devices or zones
> of pauses, to avoid burning up . . . Last night a group
> of men were discussing the general hysteria of the
> present age; the great rapidity with which all means of
> communication have outrun the value of whatever we
> have to communicate. (I must re-read Kipling's Bandar-
> log, one of the greatest of satires.) It is even significant
> that News was once called Intelligence but not so often
> nowadays. In our anxiety to talk constantly with all
> parts of the world, by cable, radio, telephone and
> newsprint, we almost forget the best kind of talk there
> is, with one's self.[10]

Chris would not call his essay 'Epistle to the Colossians'
without good reason. In the original epistle St Paul wrote from
captivity in Rome to warn Christians in Colossus against the
danger of angel worship. Sovereignty in the universe came
from God and His Son through whom they had received the
gifts of the Spirit. The role of angels was subordinate. In
another essay by Chris called 'Mind Erosion':

> The magnificent achievements of science have also
> raised up devils to plague us, principalities and powers
> we have not learned how to control. I mention only
> one, of such terrific scope that it reaches from zenith
> to pit and is efficient in both regions: the great life-
> giving and destroying angel, Publicity. People can be
> killed with photographs as surely as with guns. The

arts are encouraged by reasonable publicity, but they
need privacy too.[11]

In his 'Epistle to the Colossians' Chris was warning against the
worship of Publicity. The threat to society was often not wilful
wickedness but mere thoughtlessness. The essay on 'Mind
Erosion' carried a further message:

> Now the concern that occupies my own mind is that
> never anywhere, at any time was secluded creative
> thinking so difficult to achieve as in America today.
> Every human being is endowed with a limited and
> infinitely precious stock of attention power; and life
> today is such that – unless the individual is singularly
> obstinate and cunning – the native and tender inno-
> cence of the mind, the artist's birthright, is dissipated
> or conventionalised by endless, incessant competitive
> demands. By newspapers, by electric lights, by tele-
> phone, by radio, by moving pictures, by airplane and
> motor car and church and school and State, by a thou-
> sand appeals, admonitions and interruptions the mind
> is assailed and distracted. When the time comes to
> throw the whole power of one's will into some superb
> task, too often we find our faculties grown brittle or
> callous by repeated overstimulus. We hear a good deal
> about the agricultural problems of soil erosion . . .
> surely not less serious is the matter of mind erosion:
> the dust storms of daily excitement and triviality can
> easily blow away the sensitive topsoil of the spirit.

In this essay Chris told for the first time the story of 'the
telegram my mathematical friend [Bucky] received from a
distinguished artist' [Isamu Noguchi]:

A distinguished artist visiting in Mexico City was lately

commissioned to do a symbolic mural for a government building. The Mexican ministry of art desired the painting to be modernist in style, and the artist decided to attempt in the central panel some graphic suggestion or representation of the Theory of Relativity. My mathematical friend received from the artist the following telegram: 'Send by return wire intelligent statement of Einstein Formula.' My friend with heroic patience condensed the necessary equations and assumptions into a Western Union Day Letter. Even under the most savage compression it cost him over $10. I rather suspect the receiving office in Mexico City may have imagined it to be some sinister diplomatic or capitalistic code. I have a copy of that telegram and cherish it as a historic document.[12]

The mural by Isamu Noguchi shows a Mexican child gazing at the formula $E = mc^2$ taken from Bucky's telegram of explanation. Above a window is a moving piece of sculpture showing an infant in the moment of birth. The mural symbolises humanity giving birth to the child for whom $E = mc^2$ is the vision of the future.[13]

Chris did not quote the telegram but used the fact that such vital information could be conveyed in a day letter telegram as an example of streamlining to be compared with Thomas Wolfe who had written a million words yet felt he had only just come to grips with his subject. Chris predicted a change in literary style:

I seem sometimes to discern in the work of some writers who are intuitively ahead of their generation, what I like to think of as a kind of streamline dynamics. Virginia Woolf once said that 'The novelist of the future will take reality for granted'. By that I suppose she meant that he won't waste time and energy on describing details of the furniture and scenery that the reader can well supply – would even prefer to to supply – from his own mind.[14]

Chris had been thinking of streamlining in all areas of human endeavour. Bucky recalled:

He was writing about a world that did not get stream-lined into considerable perfection but happens as yet to be exploited in unfavourable ways. Quite a fascinating thought we discussed once was that Tennyson as a poet lived very close to the time that scientists discovered the second law of thermodynamics, namely that every system is giving off energy and thereby automatically altering the environment. Environmental changes are irreversible and irrevocable. So Tennyson in *Morte d'Arthur* said 'The old order changeth yielding place to new' and he goes on 'as God fulfils himself in many ways lest one good custom should corrupt the world'. He could see that as people brought things to perfection they'd say 'this is something to hold on to' but change is inevitable and people holding on to things only means damming up the stream and then a sudden burst. Revolutions come from good customs. It is the seemingly good customs, to which humanity inadvertently clings, that block evolution's inexorable changing and inevitably produce revolution.[15]

4

Image or Invention

Chris tried his own hand at a streamlined novel when he wrote *The Trojan Horse*. The technique foreshadowed the immediacy which radio, then television, would have when commentaries on major events in the world came into one's sitting room as readily as the changing fortunes of two football teams in a big game. Chris never said what his 'Trojan Horse' symbolised but implied it was Power gone out of control. He sent Bucky a copy of a letter which he circulated privately to explain his intentions:

> And the horse itself? Ha, maybe you'll have fun identifying what that discomforting quadruped means. Do you see its horrid blank face leering over the walls of our little fortified civilisation? Is it War, or is it the Machine? Or is it Science, or Fascism, or Communism, or Power in the general? At any rate as Cassandra truly says 'Power, the useful brute, is past control . . .'
>
> At the beginning we see war burlesqued on the level of a college football game, and they are all taking it seriously at that level. But toward the end we begin to see that the siege is a mighty serious thing; and even poor Troilus is aware of the horror of the gas masks and the 'insect troops'. Human absurdities (our own included) are not likely to be mended; they require both laughter and scourging; but I think it is best for the

laughter to come first. The first thing that will startle the reader will be the affront of modern argot in the mouths of those traditional characters . . . Chaucer, I knew, would approve. That was the way he worked. He was never afraid of humanity's two great interlocking privileges, the beautiful and the absurd. I put it this way to Chaucer when we were talking:–

> Let us not forget the comic
> With us, laughter is atomic.[1]

Bucky recalled:

When Chris talked of laughter being atomic he was thinking of incredible energy – of the explosiveness of laughter. He made that remark before there was atomic energy. There was the idea that the atom could be split but it hadn't been accomplished, so it was quite an extraordinary statement. Chris also foresaw the TV of today when at that time we only had radio. He made the radio commentary much more extreme than anything we had then and when World War II came along it began to happen. He really anticipated it in a big way.[2]

Chris had sensed the vital role radio would have when war came. He wanted to shock the reader by comparing the unreality of war at a distance with its horror when experienced first-hand. Bucky's recollection was that in this novel Chris was exploring political ideas whereas he, himself, was apolitical. New artefacts would make old problems obsolete. While Chris worked on *The Trojan Horse,* Bucky revived his Dymaxion bathroom:

During the time I was at Phelps Dodge I produced a

second round of prototypes of my 1927 Dymaxion bathroom. Bathrooms require large amounts of copper tubing, other fixtures and wiring which run through the buildings and out to the main water supplies and sewerage systems. Since Phelps Dodge was then the third largest copper producer in the world, development of a complete mass production bathroom which could be installed like a large icebox and connected to the main (service) lines was highly desirable as a tenant's property unit . . . The bathroom had economic potential to Phelps Dodge. I made twelve prototype bathrooms of copper because copper is easy to heat and anneal and keeps its form. My idea was that ultimately they would be made of reinforced plastic . . . Metal would not do except for the prototype. It was too cold.[3]

During this time Bucky was also working on his book called *Nine Chains to the Moon*. His belief that Einstein's theory had opened up remarkable possibilities for improvements in domestic life style was a basic theme. $E = MC^2$ was 'Mrs Murphy's horse power'. Bucky has recorded in his autobiography the story of how he came to have an interview with Einstein about the book.[4] He chose the title because he wanted to make the moon seem nearer in time and space. He had worked out mathematically that if every person on earth stood on another's shoulders they would form a chain long enough to reach the moon nine times. Many of the ideas in *Nine Chains* had been discussed with Chris and Bucky gave Chris the credit for its publication:

The book was taken on by Lippincott entirely on Chris's say-so, my first published book.[5]

One of Bucky's deductions was that Einstein's original concept of time had derived from his experience as a patent

examiner in Switzerland where everyone was trying to make
a new and better chronometer:

> I was sure that Einstein's idea about Newton's concern
> for exact time permeating the universe was influenced
> by empirical proof that no man had accurate proof of
> time . . .

This theory of Bucky's had a curious parallel in a comment
made by Chris in his World's Fair essay in 1936 where he
described a visit to a watch factory:

> I brought away with me a box of tiny assorted parts –
> miniscule cogs and wheels and spindles, starry spores
> and germs of TIME. I felt in this prickly debris, pawn-
> broken jewellery of the moment, was something
> mortal. A lesson if I were nimble enough to get it. But
> I am always at the foot of my own class. It was an
> Inside Job for the mind, too far in. I couldn't put them
> together, even mentally into one conscious tick.[6]

Bucky was interested in Chris's interpretation of an 'Inside Job
for the mind, too far in':

> I have found the words 'in' and 'out' very extraordi-
> nary as they have different meanings than just opposite
> directions. I was thinking about this in connection with
> Chris's phrase. If you are faithful to my principle that
> you should never say 'down' or 'up' but always 'in' or
> 'out', 'instairs' and 'outstairs' instead of 'downstairs'
> or 'upstairs', you will gradually get the sense that you
> are indeed living on a planet, a spaceship.[7]

In *John Mistletoe* Chris had spoken of 'the insides of
things' quoting a conversation with Kipling about *Thunder on*

the Left although he did not mention Kipling by name:

> One of the greatest and boldest of living authors once
> said to him: 'What a fool you were to write that book;
> *what* a fool! How you will regret it presently. Thank
> God I always had sense enough not to try to write
> about the insides of things. Why did you do it?' The
> younger man, rather startled, could only say: 'I had to.'
> The other looked at him penetratingly, his eyes very
> bright under thick juts of eyebrow. His voice changed.
> 'Was it laid upon you? It was. Don't attempt to deny
> it! – Then I understand perfectly.'[8]

Certainly both Chris and Bucky sensed the importance of 'the
insides of things', but in different ways. Chris's inward thinking was not geometric structure. He projected himself inwards
to discover his identity and kept finding layer after layer of
personality. As Bucky put it:

> *Inward Ho!* epitomised this aspect of Chris. As he
> thought inwardly to the microcosm he would reach the
> infra-tunable. I was projecting myself inwards and
> outwards to find more and more principles of the
> universe, their primitive conceptualities and their objec-
> tive realizations in time.[9]

Unquestionably Bucky's dedicated study of Einstein's theories
contributed to the development of his own.

Bucky had also begun serious work on ideas connected
with the map of the world:

> At that time my map was an intuitive way of looking
> at the Earth which I felt could be derived from exact
> mathematical processes . . .
>
> My thought about the map was that it was very

important how man sees the Earth, I wanted to develop a means of simultaneously seeing the whole Earth without visible distortion of the relative shape or size of any of the parts as in Mercator. What I did was take the 90th meridian of longitude instead of the equator for the basis of my projection. This produced a map which showed the Earth from a different vantage point. This map was the main scenic backdrop for *Nine Chains to the Moon*.

Chris was very excited by my discoveries and encouraged me to go on working on *Nine Chains* and then when it was accepted for publication he did everything he could to get publicity for it.

My geometry was beginning to take shape also. I had the idea of the Vector Equilibrium when I first close-packed twelve unit radius spheres radiantly or gravitationally arrayed around the central sphere which I felt was the basic nuclear pattern in Nature. Then I did the 'jitterbug' model.[10]

In those days 'jitterbugging' was a new kind of dance, where people took up a succession of different positions. Bucky's model was a geometric shape which could transform itself progressively from a tetrahedron to what he called a Vector Equilibrium, a polyhedron with six square faces and eight triangular ones. Bill Baird, who designed a model polyhedron from the end-papers of *Nine Chains*, later used Bucky's 'jitterbug' as a puppet on TV. He called the puppet 'Pumper' because the inward and outwards pulsing of the vectors was like a pumping operation as the shape contracted and expanded symmetrically. Bucky recalled telling his patent attorney about the Vector Equilibrium when he had the model with him at Grand Central Station:

I remember we were going upstairs to the balcony and

we stopped at the stairway's mid landing and I talked Vector Equilibrium. I had all the mathematics at this time. And he said, 'You can't patent a principle of nature but you can patent a unique application of the principle. I think we could take your map and use it to demonstrate your unique application of a nature principle.' So he made the map patent the basis of the application . . . It took nearly ten years with special pleas and many official appearances at the U.S. patent examiner's office before they granted my patent claims. I must have talked to Chris about all these synergetic events from the very beginning of our friendship.[11]

Chris meantime was editing *Bartlett's Familiar Quotations* with Louella Everett. The balance of forces and tensions with which Chris was concerned were quite different to Bucky's, as shown by his Preface. No patents involved here.

What makes words memorable? It would be useful if we knew, but I doubt we ever shall. The subtle adhesions of adult memory are unintentional and unconscious; that is the true Learning by Heart we were told of in school, when they really meant Learning by Rote. Grown minds have an abated regard for the operations of conscious intelligence. We have found (in many a secret surprise) that the images which sink deepest are often those we scarcely knew, at the time we were noticing at all. Like a skilful diver they went through the outer film of sense with very little splash.

The mind has a delicate property of surface tension, a restricting and tightening function, which creates a superficial envelope against too easy interruption or dispersion of the precious Me within. Whatever somehow punctures that protection is latent for memory. All we dare say about it is that it satisfies some inner necessity of our own. It is most likely to be metrical because we are so ourselves. Well did the word <u>incantation</u> meaning 'speech singable' come to assume the suggestion of witchcraft. One can melodise words without stopping to consider how silly they are. Who cares?

> *The magic happens –*
> *It creeps into your mind, you find it here.*
> *You are my poem then, for in my heart*
> *Lovelier than a sonnet, you made rhyme*
> *And I had memorised you unaware.*

No poet was in the least astonished by Professor Einstein's pronouncements about the relativity of Time. We knew it always: here is Chaucer thinking the very thoughts that came to us, so hot and immediate and self-englamoured today of days. It is not we who think life but life that thinks us . . .

The poets are the most savage historians. There have been plenty who thought 'The world falls asunder, being old,' and ends 'not with a bang but a whimper . . .'[12]

The work on Bartlett was completed in the spring of 1937 and *The Trojan Horse* during summer. During the autumn Chris's father died. He had been a well-known figure in the American Mathematical Society serving once as President. But he never gave up his British citizenship and retained always the reticence of an English Quaker. Thanks to long university vacations he and our grandmother had been able to spend a lot of time in England. From now on Chris went more frequently to Baltimore to visit his mother.

At the end of the year the death of Chris's old friend Don Marquis also affected him profoundly. Don had had a big influence on Chris's development as a writer. His entertaining columns in which Archie, the cockroach, and Mehitabel, the ex-theatre cat, exchanged ideas were extremely popular. Chris admired Don and at one stage they collaborated on a novel, *Pandora Lifts the Lid* (1924). Not long after Chris and Bucky had their first meeting, Don suffered a paralytic stroke. Chris was very shocked by the appalling consequences of this illness and undoubtedly had a sense of foreboding about it. He spoke at Don's funeral – and wrote afterwards:

> Don Marquis was . . . a deeply mercurial intuitive artist and passionately concerned with the ardors and problems of art. A human being so largely and kindly planned moves always in widening rings of irony. It was tragic to realise that he who uttered so many genial shouts in praise of idleness, was actually broken by overwork. He was, if I ever saw one, a victim of the constantly tightening strain and pressure of our present way of living. There was in the last two years (after a cerebral stroke) nothing left of him but the look in his eyes, and it was grim to speculate how much he realised of what had happened. I cannot help thinking that he had a very special message to younger artists, a message which was implicit in many of his seemingly jocular paragraphs. It was this: Energy is not endless, better hoard it for your own work. Be intangible and hard to catch, be secret and proud and inwardly unconformable. Say yes and don't mean it; pretend to agree; dodge every kind of organisation, and evade, elude, recede. Be about your own affairs as you would forbear from others at theirs, and thereby show your respect for the holiest ghost we know, the creative imagination.[13]

Bucky recalled:

> It was New Year's Eve the day of Don's funeral and afterwards those present went on to drink a good many whisky sours at Rothmans and to talk about Don. It was the beginning of a tradition we maintained afterwards each time a special friend died.[14]

5

Expectation Season

1938 was the year in which Chris and Bucky saw the most of each other. Bucky was 'between jobs' and able to travel regularly with Chris. During the spring, in between trips, he managed to arrange for one of his prototype bathrooms to be delivered to the Morley home in Roslyn, Long Island. It was installed in Chris's writing cabin called the Knothole, located in the adjacent woodlot. It remains today as one of the features of the Knothole which was moved to the Christopher Morley Park in Nassau County, Long Island, in 1966.[1]

The two men were so frequently together that there was no correspondence except for the occasional notes like this one:

March 20, 1938

Bucky! God Bless!

I am just leaving Chi for Galesburg.
It is extremely important to know when you can get to Chicago. Can you let me know? Can you make it next Saturday & Sunday? Address c/o Hotel Custer, Galesburg, Chris[2]

A number of the trips on which the two men travelled together were to the Middle West, which Bucky particularly enjoyed because he had lived there when he first began developing his ideas. Chris gave him a book of verse he'd written called *Old Loopy*, 'for R.B.F. 1) because he loves Chicago, 2) to remind him of the New Moon feeling, 3) for Shakespeare's birthday, April 23, 1938'. Bucky recalled:

> At that time Chris had begun to collect data for *Kitty Foyle* and he was particularly interested in what women said and did. Whenever he heard or saw anything of interest he was in a hurry to write it down. He had a great many women friends in a great many places who always made him really their own. He gave himself completely to them when he was with them. I don't think he could have been the writer he was if he hadn't been the human being that he was. I knew him very intimately as we travelled around. He had so many lecture engagements that he had to have someone to make the arrangements. He called me his Duenno.[3]

Chris later utilised experience and information assimilated from talking to friends and to students on Middle West campuses for some of the background to his novel. The most hilarious trip to Chicago, however, was one arranged by Chris with the deliberate intention of providing publicity for Bucky as well as himself. The two men travelled from New York in the engineer's cab of the new streamlined Broadway Limited on its first trip from New York to Chicago for the Pennsylvania Railroad. As it stopped in Philadelphia, by pre-arrangement, Bucky was handed the galley proofs of *Nine Chains* while he and Chris leaned out of the cab wearing engineer's caps and had their photographs taken.

Just before this Chicago trip Chris recorded in his diary that he and Frank Henry (Lippincott editor) had decided 'corner of 45th and 5th that her name was Kitty Foyle!' Later in Chicago at one of their parties Chris read some of the novel aloud to get reactions – 'Bucky grieved by K.F.', he noted. Chris anticipated that there would be controversy about the book. From the outset he had determined to write it in the first person as a woman.

The various parties generated a lot of publicity for Bucky although Chris was in Chicago for a series of autographing sessions for his own books. He recorded in his diary brief but cryptic allusions to their activities. They were interviewed by several different journalists, entertained by Vincent Starrett, author and critic, and by Narcissa Swift, a mutual friend. She enjoyed their company so much that she travelled back to New York with them. When Bucky had a party in their hotel room, twenty people came and Chris stated laconically 'bed broke'.[4]

On their return Bucky started a new job at *Fortune* Magazine. Experiencing the heady delights of authorship he made a number of changes when he received the page proofs of his book and incorporated twenty-two prognostications for the future:

> I'd been making forecasts for a long time and finding that people didn't give me any credit for forward thinking. So I took out one whole chapter and up in front where I knew the reviewers would look I put twenty-two predictions of what was going to happen in the next ten years.

Some of Bucky's prognostications still make interesting reading through they were not repeated when the book was reissued in 1963. One was certainly fulfilled very shortly – that advanced arts such as radio and aviation would 'traffic' across the pole. The forecast that the stock exchange would be completely mechanised and popularly employed worldwide has taken longer. A number disregarded political realities. An example: Bucky's belief that 'the governments of the

U.S., Canada and Russia and primarily all cold or high countries will become industrial democracies socialising all industries in the plenitudinous categories evoluting as severely competitive in all the scarcity categories with no artificial legislative manipulations of the respective status-quo of these categories'.[5]

Throughout the time that *Nine Chains* was at the printers, Chris's diary indicated that he and Bucky were meeting three or four times a week on one ploy or another. Their most important trip in 1938 was a vacation. Bucky and Chris decided to go off on a jaunt together when both their families were having holidays elsewhere. On some distant occasion in his past Chris had worked out that men born in Pennsylvania in 1890 could expect to live until they were 48.32 years old. He had calculated that this event would take place in his own life in July 1938. Bucky recalled:

> Chris called our trip together Expectation Season because he had reached the age that life insurance actuaries said was his life expectancy, or he thought he had.

Later, in *History of an Autumn,* Chris commented:

> I had reckoned that anything that happened to me after meridian July 28 was beyond Expectation; and that from then on I would be what I have always been in my heart, a poet. I don't mean in any trivial sense of rhyming and versing. I mean in trusting more to intuition and less to argument.

Bucky recalled:

> I met Chris off a train in Albany because I had just taken Anne and Allegra to Lake Placid for a few days.

I had a brand new car. Later he christened it Ten Eyck for Albany's Ten Eyck Hotel where we had lunch before setting forth. We wanted to see various places in New England like the Green Mountains, the White Mountains, places like Kipling's old home in Brattleboro, Vermont.

We did all sorts of things on that trip and various people who lived locally joined us as we went along. In the evenings we planned to read aloud so we brought books along for that. Chris brought John Donne.[6]

Chris's diary of the events and activities was written retrospectively and gave a racy account of the adventures which ranged from playing ski-ball and listening to five cent records of Flatfoot Floogie to discovering a statue of R. Burns in Montpelier, Vermont, and a memorial table to the 'sleeping sentinel' pardoned by Abraham Lincoln. Towards the end of the trip Bucky slid down the artificial ice chute at the Coconut Grove in Boston. In Boston they also went to the Public Gardens and had a trip in a swan boat. They drove to Cambridge to visit the home of Bucky's illustrious ancestor, Margaret Fuller. They had a look at 9 Hollis Hall where Bucky's great-grandfather had roomed in 1799, and, by coincidence, Bucky's brother, Wolcott, in 1921. The party returned to New York, as one could still do in those days, by steamboat from Boston, drinking New York State champagne which Chris had seen advertised 'For Life's Great Moments'.

But of the really 'great moments' on their trip very little was said in the retrospective diary. On Saturday 30 July, they were driving round to find a place to stay and 'halted up the Wild Ammonoosuc River (after the covered Bdge at Sweetwater)'. It was at Ammonoosuc that the reading party took place.

There were a few scribbled notes in Chris's diary which were written on the spot and at the time:

I drink the, of yr youth

———

Under the press of multitude &
They fled to Ammonoosuc
hot stone
pink blossom
No other river shall surpass the
stripling Ammonoosuc

What shall you find, a fallen ash
golden water pouring down,
throw love, radiant energy, luck
into the melting pot
turned the world to nobler
came & went like shapes of laughter.
  Rainbow Café at Whitefield
Beside the Ammonoosuc win
Take all the shapes of fear and sin
And pour the Ammonoosuc in.[7]

A happy accident had led the reading party to a place which perfectly echoed their mood. Bucky described it:

> We spent two nights at Ammonoosuc. There were two rivers that met, and a pond, later called Egg Nog Pond. It was a truly lovely spot. I can't remember what we read aloud exactly. I know we were thinking a lot about time and the mystery of life in time. When I wrote *Nine Chains* I thought our sense extension into radiation might mean we would discover the answer to the mystery of life in time. Now I know we won't. The more we know the more we realise how little we know. Some things we're not meant to understand. But we were exploring really important ideas at Ammonoosuc. Chris had raised a lot of them in his writing.[8]

49

These passages from *Where the Blue Begins* illustrate what Bucky had in mind:

> My mathematics is very rusty, he [Mr Gissing] said to himself, but I seem to remember something about *locus* which was a curve or a surface every point of which satisfied some particular equation of relations among the coordinates. It begins to look as though life might be a kind of locus whose commanding equation we call God. The points of the locus can't conceive of it because of course it has no existence save as a law of their being. It exists only for them; they only by it. But there it is – a perfect, potent, divine abstraction.
>
> Mr Gissing was acutely conscious of Time . . . After a period in which time ran by unnoticed he would suddenly realise a fresh <u>Now</u> and feel uneasy in the knowledge that it would shortly dissolve into another one. He tried vainly, to swim up-stream against the smooth, impalpable, fatal current. He tried to dam up Time, to deepen the stream so he could bathe in it carelessly. Time, he said, is life; and life is God; time then is little bits of God. Those who waste time in vulgarity or folly are the true atheists . . .[9]

In *Nine Chains* Bucky had spoken of Einstein's theory of relativity as a 'concept of Universe, all parts of which are in constant motion . . . a concept of LIFE as TIME itself, the first new thought of cosmic character to emerge since 200 B.C. Time was first mentioned as an entity by Sappho and from Sappho's day the idea was kept alive by poets'.[10]

In *Inward Ho!* Chris had claimed that poetry dealt with essences which were perpetually in motion. [See the quotation at the beginning of Chapter Three.]

Bucky recalled:

We were thinking intuitively. We talked E.S.P. at this time. Incidentally the American Academy of Science has now yielded on this. They concede that the evidence is overwhelming. We discussed it deliberately because we were certain that there were laws operating in the universe manifesting themselves, which had not as yet been identified. We looked for laws – and the only regularities we could discover were those such as the inter moon-sun gravitational pulling of the planet Earth's ocean tidal patterns and the moon phase of twenty-eight days and the menstruation cycle of women which is related to 'moons', 'months'. We felt these might be typical of the inter-synchronised rhythms of bodies in the universe. The Earth and the Moon and Earth's peoples, seasons and protoplasmic cells were part of a bigger cosmic resonance pattern. Since the word 'month' is related to the moon I have always taken the twenty-eight day month as funda-mental and celestial. There should be thirteen months in the year. As I've told you, we had that new moon feeling. We felt it had something to do with a periodic pull that made us feel the new moon was there.

I was particularly aware of the importance of the prime integer thirteen at this time because of the vector equilibrium. I had discovered that if you took one sphere and then packed spheres the same size tangen-tially round it as tightly as possible you always finished up with a symmetrical nucleated thirteen, one in the centre and twelve around it. Then the faces of the poly-hedron which enclosed all these spheres were the eight triangles and the six squares of the VE. So thirteen was a very significant figure in my geometry.[11]

Discussion of a cosmic religious sense and the relation of man's individual soul to the universe underlaid the

Ammonoosuc experience. Bucky was thinking about radiant energy. Chris was wondering if emotions had shape: 'came and went like shapes of laughter'. 'Take the shapes of fear and sin and pour the Ammonoosuc in.' It was after his return that he wrote the poem entitled 'Ammonoosuc':

There were two streams that bear the name,
One is the Wild and one the Tame
And on an afternoon we came
To the Wild Ammonoosuc.

We lay in stupor, sweating, prone
Upon a ledge of sunwarmed stone
I could not rest for beauty shown
Beside the Ammonoosuc.

The small pink flower on supple stalk
The confidential, water-talk
As you came down from Moosilauke
O amber Ammonoosuc.

Unspeakable in rhyme or prose
That moving Now the spirit knows.
The flow that pauses, pause that flows
So like the Ammonoosuc.

And I who had escaped from men,
From How and Why and Where and When,
Cried: Take me, make me whole again,
O blessed Ammonoosuc.

Where her crystal overran it
I lay down in channelled granite
Braced against the pushing planet
I bathed in Ammonoosuc.

In that sluice of stream and sun
I dreamed that I and everyone
A whole new ethic had begun
   Inspired by Ammonoosuc.

Refreshed in her, I understand
One truth from A to ampersand
That every heart in every land
   Has its own Ammonoosuc.

Be then, O secret cataract,
For me both parable and fact;
You gave me what my courage lacked
   O reckless Ammonoosuc.

The open way has symbols three:
The fire, the stream, the growing tree;
If I grow morbid, say to me
   Remember Ammonoosuc.[12]

6

Rededicate

At the end of his brief holiday Chris returned to Roslyn. The family was still away so he was on his own. Now that the shadow line of life expectancy had been crossed there was a change of perspective in Chris, but it came gradually and not too easily. In his diary:

> *August 9, Tuesday*
> Now that actuarial Expectation is over, try to make this surplus count for joy, beauty, kindness and courage. Bucky spent last night with me: he grew eloquent in insistence that I must make some big contribution; not laugh and evade, he said. How lovely he was, walking to and fro in flux of words. About 3 a.m. he woke with a nightmare, dreamed he was in a plane. He cried 'But you'd look sweet/Upon the seat of a cockpit built for two . . . But don't let her take the controls.'
>
> What a moonlight, painfully dazzling, when Bucky and I sat out by the rock in the garden – alongside the sundial – and drank a mild gin and ginger.
> 'Too bright for my eyes.'[1]

Bucky was very moved to see the diary:

> I have said Chris was a very great scholar. He had a deep understanding of life, an extraordinary sensitivity

54

toward all human beings and I told him that I felt he had been having his fun with his belly laughs and his Shakespearean jokes, that he'd been doing that and doing it superbly but the time had really come for him to use his wisdom in a large scale undertaking. He was needed in a more direct way. That's what we talked about that night. That led I think to his getting out his next book *History of an Autumn* (1938) but he felt he still wasn't influencing people as he should.[2]

Bucky's comments that night had affected Chris deeply:

> *August 11, Thursday*
> All day yesterday I groped for the Word. I read Enid Bagnold's fine book, *The Door of Life*. I drove away the dogs who were hankering for Corky. I mowed the front lawn. (Bucky left at 10 a.m. and I was alone all day.) I was uneasy – almost desperate with brooding, groping, delaying. I soaked in a hot bath about 6 p.m. – made myself toast and soft boiled eggs. It poured rain as usual. I woke at 3 a.m. and one word was in my mouth REDEDICATE.[3]

Within a few days Chris had written his poem 'Ammonoo-suc'.

It was not long after their return that Chris reviewed in his column in the *Saturday Review* a book called *The Serial Universe* by J.W. Dunne. The subject matter clearly related to what they had been discussing on the reading party and Chris quickly brought the book to Bucky's attention. Bucky remarked that this had been another coincidence because he had been introduced to Dunne's earlier work by the engineer who had designed the Dymaxion engine. Dunne's theory of a series of time fluxes was similar to Bucky's in that it was structural but the pattern was rectangular. Bucky explained this:

He had a precessional view and worked in parallel lines. But at that time they hadn't made the discoveries they have now in optics with the wide angle lens. We see divergently but think we see parallel.[4]

The Dunne theory can be used to explain precognitive dreams, a phenomenon which Chris had described in his essay on 'The Sense of Significance':

On a great spread of beach at low tide; a warm vacant afternoon, the smell of hay blowing down from the cliffs mixed with the strong acid of the sea. Far above, continual twitter of larks, the ear unconsciously sharpening itself to follow their wiry tinkle to the height where it blurs with your own blood stroke. In that sunny vacuum of feeling, a chime from the church a mile away. The wave of deep sound booms overhead. Then, after the passage of the note, a smaller following vibration, an actual quaver of air felt rather than heard, a magically secret ripple in the blue, the gently churning wake of those thick pushing clangs. That infinitesimal tremble swimming in soft space, was like hearing the actual movement of some strange law of life. A French lady told me the other day on that beach, in a certain slope of sunlight, she had seen one of the bathers apparently surrounded by a halo of brightness. I know that one afternoon I went far along the coast, toward a weather beaten house that stands solitary by the sea. It had beckoned me since I first saw its outline in the distance. When I got near it I recognised it at once. I had seen that same house, or at least one sufficiently like it, a year before, in a dream.[5]

Further discussions along these lines were now deferred while Chris set to work seriously on *Kitty Foyle*. In his diary he noted:

Exceptionally beautiful day.

Subconsciously all my thought tending to the problem of Kitty Foyle.

How to do her justice.

As I have often said to myself 'She is not my type'. I mean I do not believe I myself would be likely to penetrate her armor of reserve (which is considerable). This may seem absurd since she has no existence except in my mind. Yet not so absurd either. A fairer way to put it, I don't think she would care for me. The created thing has its own rights even against its own creator.[6]

No matter how many people gave him insights Kitty Foyle was a fictional character and not based on any one individual. Chris also referred in his diary:

Kitty Foyle unconscious observer telling things simply as she sees them, unaware of the depth of idiosyncrasy, kindness and courage of her seeing – begin story ½ way through as one does in a movie.[7]

Chris had now begun to expound the idea that if women had more say in the management of affairs and were willing to be ruled by their natural instincts perhaps the world would be a better place. He wanted Kitty Foyle to enunciate important truths without being aware of their significance and he wanted some of her background to contrast sharply with the social stratification of the Eastern seaboard. He deliberately set out to write a book about a type of woman who had not previously had a role in fiction. He invented a name for her – white collar girl.

The importance of women's contribution to events however was to stem rather from their intuition than from rational reactions – an attitude which would not find favour with supporters of women's lib.

Later in the summer Bucky must have been wondering about whether he was fully exploiting his own resources. The result, another jaunt, this time at his suggestion. Chris's diary:

> *August 23 (Tuesday 8½ p.m.)*
> Yesterday . . . Bucky Fuller telegraphed me from Philadelphia, met me at Gotham Book Mart 6 p.m., we drove up Riverside Drive, Henry Hudson Parkway, Sawmill & Cross County & Hutchison River Parkways to new Merritt Parkway which took us (with glorious pile up clouds of sunset) all the way to Norwalk – got to Southport (Tide Mill Inn) about 8.30. Had Jameson Irish whiskey on porch over water, then to Bridgeport, dinner at Schnitzelbank Restaurant & to Bucky's old Dymaxion factory. Spent night at Tide Water: this morning picked flowers, had a swim left lovely little Southport about one o'clock, caught 2 p.m. ferry (the old Tudicum) at Stamford.[8]

Chris loved the car ferry across Long Island South. Before the parkways it had meant he could get to New England without driving through New York City. The trip to Bridgeport was to investigate the possibility of using Bucky's old factory for the manufacture of Dymaxion bathrooms and Chris recorded that Bucky had not been to the factory for three or four years as it was associated in his mind with his financial difficulties. But the name Dymaxion was still on the building and the old night watchman remembered him with joy.

The pressure of work had now increased for Chris and he found it impossible to join Bucky for a trip to Maine. This time he wrote a letter of explanation:

> *Sept 1, '38*
> Dear Old Buckling: Just a line in haste, I'm on a stump with hell's own lot of reading to get done before the Bk

of Month mtg tomorrow. I just wanted to warn you, to avoid any special disappointment, I'm afraid honestly afraid, there is no chance of my being able to make the Bear Island trip this time. And that's more disappointment to me than it could possibly be to anyone else. But honestly I'm in the vise. Young Chris goes away next Tuesday and my only chinaman's chance of financing that is to get my various odd jobs finished so I can cash them in Tuesday. I won't bore you with details but this very weekend is a turning point for all sorts of work for me, and also I do feel that even if it's only taking them off for a picnic at Lloyd's Neck I must do something for the family on Monday (Labor Day).

Don't forget that Steloff [Frances Steloff of The Gotham Book Mart] is planning a publication day shindy for 9/chains for next Thursday: maybe we can work in a snort or so after that. By then, please God, I ought to see daylight through some fiscal chinks! So bless your old heart, and all my affectionate thanks to Rosy for asking me. If when you call I truly think I can't make it, don't try too hard to persuade me. In a hurry, but God bless!

(Steloff wants you to be sure to let her know any special pals of yrs who shd be there) . . . Meanwhile over weekend I'll get something started on The Proud Shirtfront.⁹

The Proud Shirtfront was a story with I know a Secret characters which Chris had written especially for Allegra Fuller and which she had illustrated with her mother's help.¹⁰ The story had been published without illustrations earlier in the Saturday Review, and further possibilities were being considered by the two men. Chris had built the story around Bucky's recycling of the packaging which the laundry provided in shirts which they returned to him. Allegra had used the shirt boards for her first paintings. Bucky had now started an enormous clipping file of technological and scientific articles from the newspapers, which he pasted on the boards. But the publication of *Nine Chains* was uppermost in their minds. Unfortunately, although it was widely reviewed, the charts which were to be incorporated had been left out in some copies. All copies were then withdrawn and by the time they reappeared the impetus of the first publicity had dissipated. During the intervening period of several weeks there was first the severe 1938 hurricane which did great damage to New York, New Jersey and Connecticut. Then, far worse, the Munich Crisis and deep concern about the prospect of world war.[11]

Chris returned from a visit to Baltimore where his mother was seriously ill and set to work urgently on *History of an Autumn*. He dedicated it to his mother with the phrase REDEDICATE. He was irritated when people spoke of it as 'charming' or 'whimsical' – he had intended it as serious comment on events:

> I like to think that in time of such gruesome suspense there were some who had the courage to throw their own powers of luck and change and intuition into the immeasurable pot of melting. The radiation of that energy, that joy, that companionship and laughter must have its benefit however minute upon the whole level of the world's feeling.[12]

He sent a copy to President Roosevelt who wrote that he regretted not having time to read John Donne but he hoped Chris would come in some time to discuss life and literature.[13]

In spite of setbacks Chris and Bucky maintained their general high spirits so life was not being taken too seriously. Just before Christmas Chris appeared at the Gotham Book Mart with a papier mâché pig which he had commandeered

from a butcher. He did this to tease Frances Steloff because the
Gotham Book Mart catalogue referred to him as an essayist
of the stature of Charles Lamb. The pig became a familiar
occupant of the niche above Frances's desk and over the years
she persuaded many visiting celebrities to autograph it.

The two men did not travel together frequently in 1939.
Bucky's work for *Fortune* was demanding. Chris was putting
every spare moment into *Kitty Foyle*. Sometimes it was hard
to find time to meet – Chris's first diary note in that year indicated that Bucky had to join him on the train to North
Philadelphia to consult him about an article he was preparing
on cosmic thinking, in which he had mentioned Democritus,
the laughing philosopher. Chris's next communication referred
to Democritus: on a postcard from a gathering of friends
where all sent greetings because Bucky wasn't present. Chris's
message:

January 15, 1939

O Buckling!
As Democritus said:
(What did he say?) Laughter is our only weapon.
We have it here – love – from Chris.[14]

When opportunity presented itself they continued their frivol-
ities, and their occasional letters reflected this:

Weds night Feb 15

Good Buckling:
Don't be austere with me about running out on you the
other evening. I had genuine troubles to deal with out
here and it was well I did get back. I'll try to do better
when the stars and digits are in my favor, in our favor
I shd say. Bill Benet brought back to the Sat Rev office
the valentined book of his poems and I have it safe for
you. Struggling grievously with the novel; hell's tough-

ness. On enclosed slip I have typed out for Jimmy Devine that dedication. Just going to listen to that strange bird Johannes Steel on the radio to see what he has to say about our troubles.

Blessings and much love. Chris.[15]

Bucky:

Chris always listened to Johannes Steel in those days. We all listened constantly to the radio. The valentined book he mentions is very special, *Moons of Grandeur* by Bill Benet. We used to go after lunch sometimes into the Gotham Book Mart and look round. If Chris found a book he liked he would autograph it. Miss Steloff didn't mind. It was a sort of increment the purchaser got. On Valentine's Day that year we found a copy of Bill's early poems and he was with us so we all wrote in it. We wrote on several pages. I've still got it on my shelves with all Chris's books. Bill was going to become a grandfather and he was very excited. That's why we were celebrating. We were thinking of our fathers and we wrote all their initials and their college degrees and we wondered what they'd think of us. Chris wrote the page number of a poem on the flyleaf – It's Bill's poem: 'To my father' . . . 'You held life up to me like a prism.'[16]

During the early months of 1939 Chris gave a series of lectures at Adelphi College in Garden City, Long Island, near to his home at Roslyn. The series was entitled 'Literature and Companionship'. Afterwards he wrote to the president of the college and among other comments he explained why he had taken Bucky along:

It gives me a fresh futurity in my mind to think what exciting things are before you (as a college), not just behind you. That was one reason why I asked my friend, Buckminster Fuller, to talk to my literature class. I wanted them to see that there is no opposition between the arts and the sciences; they are only two adjoining sides in the polygon; a polygon which no matter how many sides we give it will never completely fill the perfect circle of knowledge. In those little spaces between the multiplying polygon and the imagined Perfect Circumstance, the poet and the artist and the post-Euclidean scientist go into their dance.

It was fun, huge fun to see the children's faces as my friend Fuller gave them an entirely new motion of a way of looking at this agitating planet – which is not itself even a Perfect Sphere.[17]

The early months of 1939 marked the real beginning of correspondence between Chris and Bucky. It became an important means of keeping in touch when they did not see each other. In April and May Bucky had begun to recognise patterns in scientific and technological progress which could be readily interpreted from his mammoth clipping file. Dorothy Thompson was persuaded to broadcast about it. Bucky also wrote to *LIFE* magazine. The letter was printed. Chris wrote to Bucky as soon as he discovered this:

10.35 p.m. June 2

I've just been out to look at the moon; a moon that would tear the balls of a brass monkey, I said to myself. I took a glass of milk and will try to ease myself on a typewriter. I wonder if I can get anywhere near the thoughts that are moving. Probably too tired; when one is tired one wonders, will the incredible morning feeling, the feeling of a fresh day after a decent sleep, that sensation of thrilling energy and amusement and a whole crowd of ideas dancing in the mind, pouring themselves into words so that you have to laugh and talk as you go along the street and you simply can't wait to get wherever it is you're going to tell someone about them . . . will that feeling ever come back again, you ask yourself, when you're tired. And on such a night, such translucence of sky and burning points of stardust and the female, female moon – she creeps up slowly here behind my big trees and torments me by the gradual swim (as Keats said).

A kind of sickness of heart to think of that moon shining on a submarine horror; the grimness of that black stern perhaps finned up above the glittering sea.

I was happy thinking about the old Buckling as I went through the new issue of *LIFE* tonight. There is an astonishing naiveté about some of *LIFE's* pronouncements; the idea that by sitting on a lawn in Iowa listening to some prof the kids can learn to write novels is adorably comic; it adds a new hell to the boblishing biz to learn that 'no less than 25 novels are being written in Iowa City'. I don't quite know how it is that things that are innocent and even helpful in themselves become at once ridiculous when gravely publicised and preached about. Together with that naiveté the *LIFE* boys are doing an increasingly excellent job. America's strength lies in exactly that naiveté; provided there are a few sufficiently acute to know it as such; and to use it as such. Very happy, I started to say, in the credit and tribute given to the Buckling. It's a pity, I suppose, that I amuse myself by such outrages of facetiousness, as today at lunch; very likely a kind of armor (as foolish as the White Knight's); it necessarily leads the casual observer to damn me as a clown; but what thrill when occasionally one encounters the observer who can read behind it. And that of course is one way of learning who are the people with whom one can be one's self. But I'm not apologising, even to myself, for putting on an act when I feel like it. It's sometimes a hell of a good act, worthwhile in itself. The proportion of solemn arses is very high in the U.S.A., especially in the learned professions. EG the Phi Beta Kappa campaign for Defense (of Intellectual Freedom!) They have sent me a booklet: 'Phi Beta Kappa Fortifies Its Sector in the Defense of the Humanities' etc. 'Membership in Phi Beta Kappa is the Apex of Achievement in America's Educational Pyramid.' The kind of people who can solemnly emit such horsewind and turtlepoop haven't even begun their secret education. Edward Everitt who made the other speech that day at Gettysburg, was probably the Phi Beta Kappa man. I'm sure Abe wasn't. (If it was Edw Everitt? Who Knows? or cares?) As I get older, and I'm getting that rapidly, I'm sure that public dinners for serious intentions are an offense and a ridicule. The only warrant for evening dress and general hells bells should be the lightest kind of apparent flippancy. (Bernard Shaw said a good thing). The great American character was once the Newly rich. Now it's the Newly Educated. It is the inferiority complex of the newly cultivated, the intellectual climbers, that gives them their passion for dressing up and going to public festivity. It is the incurable humility of some that drives them in congregations. They still are secretly astonished at being allowed to walk into the lobby of a smart hotel without being heaved out. I'm just having fun thinking about things. Trying to duck that spendthrift moonlight. In a world and time where a good deal was ugly or cruel or just plain mad what incredible beauty I have seen. How the changing shapes of man's tools and trinkets delight me. How marvellous to be old enough to remember quite different shapes of things and yet young enough in heart 'each day new Paradise to build', as the verses said which the Buckling loves to quote. A blessing on the Buckling, who might have been just a Harvard man and had so many generations of gentility and parsoonery to live down. The lining of his coat may be ragged but not the lining of his heart. The problem I face – it seemed too egoist to say it aloud in the street – is to express the very subtlest of observations through the medium (K. Foyle) of extreme simplicity; she must never be aware that she is saying important things; they are twisted out of her by accident; yes by torsion. An orange doesn't know it is so chock with vitamins and advertising merit. The Main Line was born with a silver spoon in its brains. Spaniel Smith, the Polish washerman; he moaned so when he greeted me tonight I thought at first it was he who was (as they like to say) bereaved. But he is a more educated heart than many of the Phi Beta Kappas. But he is a good man; one has to be patient with them. I must try to be patient part of the time, and to laugh in public and pray in secret. That is the best manners. Seeing the effect on most people of being grown up, I struggle against it. No, not deliberately; but I learn something of truth and beauty by not being grown up . . .

I have an anxiety to go out and have another look at that moon. Must wrestle it. It is the first night of really Hans Anderson moon which dearest L.J.M. [his mother] is dead in. The shape of trains, engines, faces in the subway; the divinely jovial hooey of advertising; a look, a flash, a silk heel in a sandal . . . 'give me what you please, I'll make it my own.' Which shall it be, moonlight or another glass of milk? Gruesome alternative. The answer should always be, both.

Oh it is our need, our tragic and secret and desperate need, that makes us vulnerable. It isn't fair to know too much about human need. What is that line in the Sonnets, 'He that hath power to hurt, and will do none . . .?' Could this evening be set to music? I must think about the sombre and ambitious Smythe. I like his looks. 'I love a look of agony because I know it's true.' But ah, the great artist keeps his look of agony inside, like the raggedness of the Buckling. Even the moon (damn her, here she blows again and sparm at that), shows us only her shining edge.

Pipe in telephone booth.

'Let me get at that.'[18]

The letter was not signed. No one else could have written it.

7

Corona Effects

In the summer of 1939 Chris completed *Kitty Foyle*, commenting that he thought of the book as a sort of feminine *Way of All Flesh*. He then felt he could take a vacation and was on a brief September visit to Lake Champlain with the family when war was declared in Europe. He wrote soon afterwards to Bucky:

> *Sept 5*
>
> Good Buckling
> Been very quiet here, either swimming or listening to radio – or even trying to think. Will be home late Friday and hope have good talk with you soon. Love, Chris[1]

It was soon clear that Chris felt events were following a pattern he had predicted in *The Trojan Horse*. He decided to rewrite the novel as a play:

> *September 19, 1939*
> Began typing out playscript of T. Horse, 12½ noon, turned on radio & heard gargling guttural & self inducted frenetics of A. Hitler. Bucky phoned about 2 p.m. to say he believed war was over 'something phony about it', cf Borah & by Sept 22 great rebalancing of power wd be evident. I said I thought the war hadn't really begun yet.[2]

'Phony War' was a phrase widely used in Britain during the early months. Other diary items had showed that Chris's attitude to World War II would be very different to that which he had held in World War I. He identified quickly with the British cause. He had not done this in 1914 even though he had just come home from Oxford. He was much more staunchly Quaker in this earlier period of his life.

September 16

In bathtub trying to consider the right course re the repeal of Arms Embargo – At length felt better by realizing that few human decisions can be absolute as betw Right & Wrong. The very act of deciding is corrupted by incidental & inherent circumstances (or innerstances) & qualifications.[3]

Sept 18

Cool & clear
2 U.S. Army planes above me as I took 8.40 a.m. train. Russian invasion of Poland. Is world revolution now the only recourse? Truth is in protective custody.[4]

Kitty Foyle was published in October. It caught on and was quickly a best seller. In the diary Chris wrote that he was 'a bit goofed by publicity'. By November there were only two cities where *Kitty Foyle* was not top best seller – Los Angeles and Atlanta, where she was beaten by Scarlet O'Hara.

What of the fundamental truths which Kitty Foyle was to enunciate without realising she was doing so? Did anyone notice? Perhaps this was part of a subconscious appreciation which readers felt. To a wide public *Kitty Foyle* was a thoroughly readable novel because the character of Kitty was extraordinarily real. How could a man penetrate so deeply into a woman's thoughts? This was the frequent comment.

There were underlying meanings which related to the discussions which Chris had had with his friends at Ammonoosuc and elsewhere. Some might have derived from John Donne's poetry, which Chris had been rereading while he wrote the book. The traditional personification of Wisdom as a woman had been renewed by seventeenth-century metaphysical posts.

Kitty Foyle later became a highly successful film. Chris with his acute ear for dialogue had assimilated a conversational style for his heroine which was contemporary. He wrote his own advertisements, describing *Kitty Foyle* as the Natural History of a Natural. Any fundamental truths which her self-musings revealed were there to be noticed as Chris preferred. They would be discovered by the reader as something familiar that he or she had always known but never expressed. Chris was not writing a treatise on metaphysics. The novel contained quite a lot of social comment. When Kitty had begun her career in the business world, selling cosmetics:

> I make my living now by trading on women's herd instincts, and I can see how useful it is for them to think they're exercising their own choices when actually they're falling in line with what some smart person has doped out for them. There are a lot more clever people in the world than you might suppose, particularly working on women; and merchandisers have learned to put ideas in people's heads without their having the slightest guess where those ideas come from. I've taught myself a lesson or I hope I have; when I find myself thinking something I stop a minute and ask myself, Now who had it all figured out beforehand that was the way they wanted me to think . . .
>
> You don't mind thinking these things to yourself. Nobody is ashamed when she's alone. How would you get in the world more of the kind of people you can feel alone with? I wonder if I could teach Mark not to tell me more than I can listen to.[5]

Kitty sacrificed her love for the Main Line hero, Wyn, in order to help him fulfil the life for which he seemed destined, one of social conformity. The question which remained for her wisdom and intuition to solve was whether Mark Eisen could provide her with a love in which she could retain her own identity. In this sense Kitty Foyle did symbolise something important in the nature of Man and Woman. It accounted for the novel's success.

Chris was not just basking in success, however. He was already beginning to brood another book:

Night of Nov 18
Very bad session of solitary despair and self scrutiny. The awful thing is never complete happiness except alone: and is literature the only cure for that? How to get that across in the book?[6]

The book he was thinking about at this time later became *The Man Who Made Friends with Himself*. He stopped work on this to produce *Thorofare* to express his Anglo-American consciousness. Another book he was making notes about was to be called *Broken English* and would reflect current misuses of the language. He was thinking ahead to his next birthday when he would be fifty:

Nov 27
Age 50. The incredible sweetness of Life so fresh & clear in mind, shd be time to write a book greatly & soberly – the moonlight tnight (2 a.m. Nov. 27) 3 stars Orion's belt violet. Mr Cassidy's house lying so silent – his first night away from home; he was cremated yestdy. [Mr Cassidy was his next door neighbour.][7]

Just before Christmas the newspapers announced that the film role of Kitty was to be taken by Ginger Rogers. On Christmas Day, in Chris's diary:

His ship came in – after years of talking about it, so suddenly he had no mooring ready.[8]

Early in 1940 Bucky completed his work for *Fortune* and after a holiday started work with the Chrysler Co. Chris utilised some of the profits from *Kitty Foyle* to purchase a house on Long Island to provide a home for wartime refugee children. He also sponsored a theatre in Roslyn for which he wrote a successful suburban comedy, which was followed by a production of *The Trojan Horse*. In the autumn when Bucky had spare time again he began writing letters on Chris's behalf about this project:

> *November 9, 1940*
> I went out to Roslyn on Long Island to see Christopher Morley's Trojan Horse present as a play at his Millpond Playhouse. I think it is wonderful. The original book, like many another clairvoyant piece, was just three years ahead of its time. I know it hurt Chris to find that so few understood its import, so vivid today. And I know that he is now elated over the understanding of the play. The understanding is mutual to both cast and audience. And the audiences are truly surprising in the off season of a distraught world . . .[9]

Shortly after this Bucky accompanied Chris on another of his lecture trips to the Middle West. With Ralph Sargent, then Professor of English Literature at Knox College in Galesburg and later Professor of English Literature at Haverford College, they went to Nauvou, Oquawka and Hannibal. Bucky recalled the incidents on this trip in considerable detail:

> The first place we went to see was Oquawka where the man who owned the first printing press on the Mississippi lived. Through correspondence this man's son had

persuaded Edgar Allen Poe to come to the Middle West to be his editor and Edgar Allen Poe was on his way there when he died. Chris wanted to find the house in case there might still be letters from Poe in the attic. We found the house, but there were no letters.

Then we went to Nauvou which was built by the Mormons and afterwards abandoned when they set off for Salt Lake City, Utah, along the Santa Fe trail. They left an extraordinary town behind with beautiful American architecture. The houses were two storeys high, very narrow, one room deep and made of stone. They looked a lot like the early Pennsylvania Dutch houses.[10]

Ralph Sargent remembered that they went to Hannibal to look at the fence which Tom Sawyer whitewashed, and decided it could do with a fresh coat. Chris bought the necessary equipment at a local store and they set to work. Bucky remembered this, but it was more important to him that Hannibal was where Chris insisted he must cross the Mississippi because in all his previous travels he had never done this. Ralph Sargent spoke particularly of the excitement which both Bucky and Chris felt when they drove round the countryside – how they enjoyed seeing the great piles of clam shells from which 'mother of pearl' buttons were cut and also their comments on the architecture. They called the style usually known as 'gingerbread' 'frozen music'. Bucky was very taken also with the corrugated galvanised granaries which were everywhere. Bucky kept talking about them and saying 'There is the house of the future.' He recalled:

It was on the trip that I saw the Butler grain bins and I was struck by the ease with which they could be converted into quite liveable fireproof huts. Nobody had thought of them as houses before. They had

Chinese hat-like conical roofs – I immediately wanted to top them with an air tight radial hemisphere dome. Because they were cylinders a domed top would be structurally stabilizing. And I would line them with insulation. Later that's what I did. The trip was a turning point in my life.[11]

During this lecture trip Chris and Bucky had begun to travel by plane. On one flight they observed 'corona effects'. These are a sort of halo around the edge of shadow. The event was recorded in Chris's diary with a diagrammatic representation signed 'R. Buckminster Fuller and C.M. vericavit'. On the next page Chris wrote:

Bucky notices corona effects around shadow of plane more brilliant behind wing.

November 19

Mild autumn brightness, flying TWA over fields of Indiana and Ohio, zigzag rail fence makes wonderful hemstitch pattern, patterns of cornshocks, trucks of yellow corn. Flew over Troy, Ohio.[12]

Bucky recalled:

I explained to Chris that corona effects proved Einstein's curved space and curved light wave theory. Looking back that incident was another reason why this particular trip seemed so important. Later when Chris and I talked about it we used to study our own shadows. Chris had noticed the halo round shadows before and wrote about it in his essay called 'The Sense of Significance'. I had noticed in my own shadow there were times when this effect was much stronger than it was at other times.[13]

Three Hours for Lunch Club, 1934. *Left to right*: Bill Hall, Max Schuster, Christopher Morley (CM), Richard Buckminster Fuller (RBF). (Courtesy Estate of RBF)

CM and RBF with Mrs Richard Bokum (Fanny Butcher), literary editor of the *Chicago Tribune*, promoting *Kitty Foyle*, November (?) 1939. (Courtesy Estate of RBF)

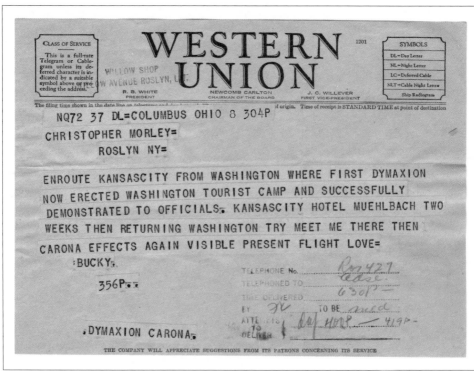

Undated telegram from RBF to CM, March (?) 1941. *See page 77.* (Courtesy HRC)

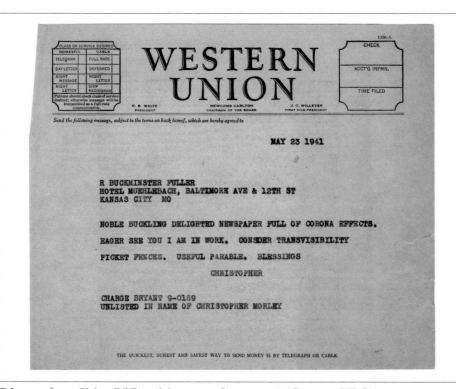

Telegram from CM to RBF, 23 May 1941. *See page 78.* (Courtesy HRC)

CM in his office in 46 West 47th Street, New York City, probably a publicity photo for *Thorofare*, November 1942. (Courtesy Estate of LMC)

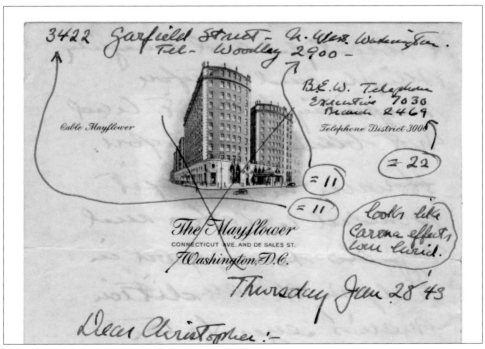

Letter from RBF to CM on using CM's expression, 'Too bright for their eyes', 28 January 1943. Note comments on corona effects and the number 22. *See page 89*. (Courtesy HRC)

Valentine card from CM to RBF, 12 February 1943. *See page 90.* (Courtesy HRC)

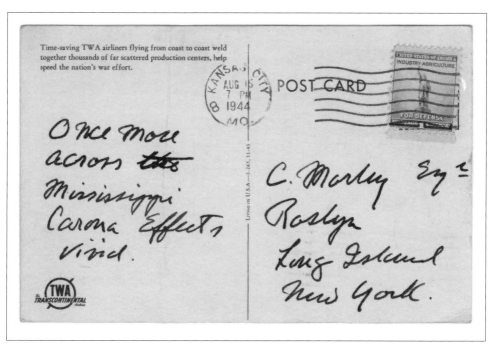

Postcard from RBF to CM on crossing the Mississippi and corona effects, 15 August 1944. *See page 120.* (Courtesy HRC)

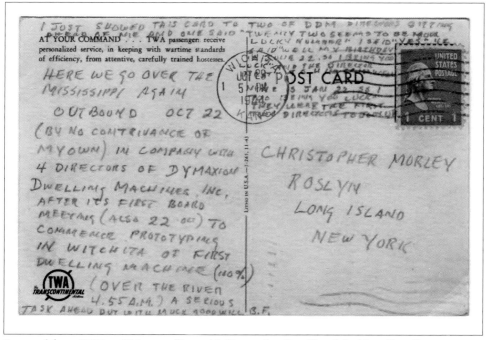

Postcard from RBF to CM: travelling with Dymaxion Dwelling Machines Inc. directors on a Twenty-two day, 22 October 1944. *See page 120.* (Courtesy HRC)

Right. Letter from RBF of 22 March 1945, a Twenty-two day. *See page 120.* (Courtesy HRC)

Below. Preparing to mail *Bartlett's Familiar Quotations,* 12th edition, 1948. *Left to right*: Elizabeth Barrett Winspear, Louis Greenfield, CM and Helen Hare. *See pages 122–125.* (Courtesy HRC)

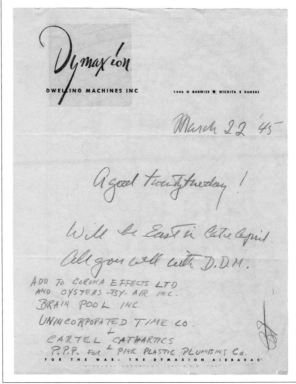

RBF at Black Mountain College, Carolina, 1948. (Courtesy Estate of RBF)

RBF's last communication to CM, 17 October 1955. (Courtesy HRC)

Chris and Bucky became very interested in this phenomenon, which they thought might reveal a universal law of nature. Studying their shadows they observed the hazy periphery which is clearly discernible on a bright day. When experiments after the war proved that the brain gives off measurable electro-magnetic energy during sleep with wave patterns related to dreams, Bucky thought this was a manifestation of the effect which he and Chris had observed. They also thought of 'corona effects' as intuitive extensions of ideas they had shared with one another. Bucky felt corona effects were operative as he made further efforts to design a new type of house:

When Chris and I returned to New York I kept on talking about the possibilities of the grain bin house. Chris sent me the money to go to Kansas City where those Butler Company grain bins were manufactured to see if I could set something up. He said 'Kitty Foyle wants to finance your going to Kansas City.' Then he sent this letter:

December 2, 1940

Dear Bucky,
The Old Man tells me to mail you this check, $150, as a foundation stone in the matter of Honeycomb Houses or Beehive Yourself. If it's a case of hives, I hope they cell!
Good luck to you in celling yourself
Sincerely yours,
HYBLA HOMES
Per (K.F.)[14]

The hexagonal structure of the honeycomb was related to Bucky's theories and one of the principles of nature which he felt should be adapted to building design – hence the puns.

The trip to Kansas City was successful. Bucky got on well

with the President of the Butler Co., who agreed to join in a 'grain bin house' project. As a result Bucky was able to find finance for the prototyping of what became the Dymaxion Deployment Unit. By February 1941 Bucky was writing Chris from Dymaxion Houses, Butler Manufacturing Company:

February 10, 1941

Dear Christopher,

Here is a little valentine souvenir from the 'Kansas Cityan' streamliner of the Santa Fe out of Chicago, 9.30 a.m. on which I arrived here January 30th. The first (Dymaxion Deployment Unit) was up when I arrived. It was very exciting but needed a number of changes to make it top notch. The newest unit will be shown in Washington to be followed by another unit in N.Y.C. Rockefeller Center and another out here – will be assembled tomorrow. It is really wonderful. We will move it east in about ten days after various tests have been applied. Expect to stop at Butler's Galesburg, Illinois factory on my way east. It is there that the Dymaxion houses will be mass produced which is really quite mystically exciting, for that is where the Nauvou trip took off from. There they will be able to produce up to 1000 a day. I will of course see Ralph Sargent if he is there. I wired him that I was coming through on the way out and suggested his coming to station platform but he received my wire too late to do so.

I saw a movie last night called 'Honeymoon for Three' all about an author on a lecture tour through Ohio, Illinois etc. His secretary with him. He had written a best seller, 'Christina' etc. Lettering looking like Kitty F. on cover. Many complications with girls who think they are Christina etc. Many incidents similar to your life. While play is extremely silly it is

still reminiscent enough to have given me a big kick
and I think it would do the same to you.
As ever,
Bucky[15]

The reply to this was a telegram:

HI BUCKLING AWFULLY PLEASED VALENTINE HOPE
EVERYTHING MOVING LOVE CHRIS[16]

The valentine was a heart cut out of the corrugated galvanised
steel sheets which were used for the houses. Bucky had the
pieces cut out and inserted bolts of the type to be used. He sent
these 'valentines' to his friends.

The film to which Bucky referred was produced by Warner
Brothers with George Brent, Ann Sheridan and Charles
Ruggles but there was no indication that Chris ever saw it.
Bucky's next message to Chris was a telegram, mysteriously
undated by Western Union:

EN ROUTE KANSAS CITY FROM WASHINGTON
WHERE FIRST DYMAXION NOW ERECTED WASH-
INGTON TOURIST CAMP AND SUCCESSFULLY
DEMONSTRATED TO OFFICIALS. KANSAS CITY
MUEHLBACH HOTEL TWO WEEKS THEN RETURN-
ING WASHINGTON TRY MEET ME THERE THEN
CORONA EFFECTS AGAIN VISIBLE PRESENT FLIGHT
LOVE BUCKY[17]

There was great optimism about the future of the house.
Robert Colgate who provided the necessary financial backing
became President of the company. Bucky was vice president.
Bucky wanted Chris to have a share of the profits because of
his initial gesture. In May he sent a postcard from a plane trip
in which he crossed the Mississippi:

Hey
Old Man
Note the speed of our expediting tail wind as we pursue the Dymaxion Trend once more to cross Nauvou and the Mississippi BUT OH VERY BUMPILY Bucky

The tail wind marked on the chart was 22, the air speed 160 mph. A letter followed:

Eve. of May 22nd, 1941

Chris,
I have wired my lawyer (brother-in-law) Bill Parkhurst, 120 Wall Street, to please expedite contract for you re earnings – if you don't hear from him soon, please call him up. All goes well . . .
I miss you
Bucky[18]

There followed a telegram from Chris:

May 23, 1941

NOBLE BUCKLING DELIGHTED NEWSPAPER FULL OF CORONA EFFECTS. EAGER SEE YOU. I AM IN WORK. CONSIDER TRANSVISIBILITY PICKET FENCES. USEFUL PARABLE. BLESSINGS. CHRISTOPHER.[19]

8

New Projections

'I am in work' meant 'I am busy'. Chris was concerned about the effect of the war on human freedom and man's intellectual capacity. He was trying to express his own views on the issues involved in the war. During the spring of 1941 he published his random thoughts on a possible updating of *The Tempest*. He felt it was a very contemporary play:

> No matter how high the intention nothing could be written *ad hoc* so moving – timely to Now as *The Tempest*. It has taken a second World War to show how apropos it is as political fugue. The full measure of its meaning needed more than three hundred years to reach its perfected felicity – or frequency. It had to wait for the invention of radio . . .
>
> The conception of Ariel as an invisible radio voice makes the fable instantly rational to our own habits of thought . . . *The Tempest* is a brainstorm or passion in the mind and the Island is the lonely island of the mind . . . it is the Island of the subconscious where the mind is getting ready to think things not yet formulated in words . . . When Ariel enters he enters in a quite different sense, not to the eye but to the ear.[1]

For Chris, Sycorax was intellectual evil which had imprisoned Ariel in a tree. Caliban was carnal evil. Prospero taught

Caliban language and made him more dangerous, so Prospero must now exploit Ariel, the spirit of Communication or Radio, to set matters to rights. Radio communication must be used to preserve the free world.

Chris also took his responsibilities as a Book-of-the-Month Club judge very seriously. Among the many books which were selected for members, Koestler's *Darkness at Noon* made a particular impact. The judges were unanimous in this selection. The novel was very important because it confronted the people of the Western democracies with a picture of brainwashing for a political motive. Those subjected to this treatment were members of the party who disagreed with changes introduced by the leadership. The book was published after the Moscow trials while Germany and Russia were still allies. A few months later Germany's invasion of Russia precipitated another complete volte-face in Communist party attitudes, similar to those Rubashov, the hero, had faithfully undergone in the early stages of his political career but could no longer support. At the end, Rubashov saw himself as a man who had lost his shadow by following every thought to its final conclusion. However, he still had a 'silent partner' whom he named his 'grammatical fiction'.

Chris doubtless appreciated the fact that Rubashov talked to his inner self as to a 'grammatical fiction', a metaphor similar to one that he himself had used in *John Mistletoe*. He felt Koestler's novel had an important message. He wrote in his review: 'This is a superb achievement . . . The kind of novel we have learned to expect from let us say Chekov or Gorki or Dostoievsky . . .'[2]

Bucky's ideas continued to take structural form. The paths of the two men had now diverged; they saw very little of each other but continued to send greetings from time to time. Bucky had hoped that his mass produced housing units would help to house people evacuated from the bombed cities of Britain. The shortage of steel made this impossible. The DDU (Dymaxion Deployment Unit) was then tested by the US Army. After Pearl Harbor, however, with the United States engaged itself in two theatres of war, rationing of essential raw materials meant that the production of the units had to be reduced and then abandoned.

During this period of strain Bucky's only letter to Chris gave no direct clue to the personal problems he was confronting. He wrote instead about Captain David Bone, who as a result of Land-Lease arrangements had been offered the command of the USS *George Washington*, the ship on which Bucky had served in the US Navy. David Bone, retired captain in the British Merchant Navy, had gone back to active service. He was an old friend of Chris's. They had met when David captained the ship which brought Joseph Conrad to the United States on his first visit as author, and Chris was one of the welcoming party. Since David Bone was a regular visitor to New York he and Bucky had come to know each other well. The letter was dated March but was not sent until July.

March 30, 1942

Dear Christopher:–

In rummaging ('Oh how I sweat when I rummage', – a new war song which we will complete together at the appropriate moment) through Dymaxion chronofile fileage I asideforthed these two sheets from a folder marked 'stationery'. I thought you might like to forward them to David Bone for they were actively virginal paper during the last phase of the 100 year civil war making our small world smaller and his fine ship larger. David has survived the tricks of the sea which are enormous but also he has survived the tricks of man. And David, a good master, is unsinkable because his life belt is fashioned with buoyant slabs of omniscient fun stoutly sewed with the canvas of integrity. While I doubt that the 'G.W.' will ever go out from

81

under him, because I know her and she has the plod-
through-on-top quality – David may say with verity
'your experience is limited, Bucky, and I have had just
such old faithfuls give me the Down express', I feel that
David will never go down involuntarily. He and his
Maker will be seeing eye to eye when David says 'Let
go all lines' for the last time. B.F.[3]

Chris was probably not aware that the DDUs were not going
well. Ultimately a small number were taken to the head of the
Persian Gulf and housed the mechanics who were responsible
for handing over to the Russians the US airplanes which were
provided for them. But in July 1942 prospects were grim after
the euphoria of the early stages of the project.

It was at this time also that Bucky decided he would give
up drinking. He had done this once before but changed course
again before meeting Chris in 1934. This time his resolve
carried through for the rest of his life. He made the announce-
ment to his family at his Silver Wedding anniversary party.
Chris and Helen had not been able to attend. They sent a
telegram of greetings:

HAPPIEST RETURNS AND CONGRATULATIONS. LOUD
CRIES OF STEWARD VERY SORRY CAN'T MAKE IT
OURSELVES CHRIS AND HELEN.[4]

Bucky recalled:

It was at this part that my own family realised for the
first time that I really had given up drinking. Shortly
after this was the only time I had any misunderstanding
with Chris. He'd begun to dislike the telephone so I
didn't like to ring him; I hadn't seen him for a long time
so I went up to his office. He was just going out to a
meeting. He probably said 'Come and have a drink',

and I probably told him I had given it up. I gave him a copy of *No More Second Hand God* and he said the title was blasphemous. But he had liked my poems when I read them out loud at Ammonoosuc. I don't think Chris ever read that book because he didn't like the title, but I only meant that everyone has to find God by his own direct experience.

I know we went out together and then when we were standing on Fifth Avenue he said something about the profits of the Dymaxion Deployment Units. Of course there weren't any. There never was anything. Bob Colgate lost a lot of money.[5]

Bucky was evidently quite hurt by this incident. It was so uncharacteristic as to be inexplicable. There was only one solution if the friendship was to continue. Bucky himself gave the answer:

Oh we put the whole thing behind us.

The next communication from Chris in Bucky's Chronofile was a page from Chris's notebook on which he had written:

My dear, he's terribly informal –
his temperament is far too thermal.
– CM, Toulemonde, 1927[6]

Chris later selected part of the poem 'No More Secondhand God' for Bartlett's *Familiar Quotations*:

Yes, God is a verb
the most active
connoting the vast harmonic
rendering of the universe
from unleashed chaos of energy . . .[7]

In the autumn of 1942 the friendship was again on a firm footing. They saw less of one another, however, so from this point on their correspondence rather than Chris's diary is the principal source of information on the interest they maintained in each other's activities for the rest of Chris's life.

Bucky's map projection had been integrated with the Vector Equilibrium (VE). The combination of the two was a demonstration of his search for a comprehensive explanation of the structure of the universe, one which would illustrate the fundamental principles of nature as he saw them. The VE had become his means of explaining the balance of interacting forces outward from the centre and inward from the surface of the sphere. This balance of forces was exploited in his design of the dome.

Bucky projected a spherical globe inward onto the Vector Equilibrium in order to have a map projection with minimum distortion. He wanted a map which could be reassembled three dimensionally or laid out flat on a plane surface in any way you wished to put the pieces together. You could then visualise much more readily the so-called 'Great Circle routes'. Great circles were geodesics and by 1942 the importance of air routes which followed them was well known to anyone with experience of air travel. Chris and his two brothers were particularly interested in this aspect of Bucky's design because of their father's research into inversive geometry. Chris's brother Felix, then the President of Haverford College, wrote to Chris, inviting him to a conference and asking him to bring Bucky with him:

Reflection has confirmed my anxiety to have Bucky Fuller bring down his devices and have them on display in one of the rooms where the attending savants can take in what he has in mind. It has a very direct bearing on the whole subject of government.[8]

Chris wrote promptly to Bucky:

September 22, 1942
9/22/1942 = 11

Buckling: This is a 22 day and a very handsome one.
Yesterday I finished correcting galley proofs of *Thorofare*. Page proofs next week. Publication, I think,
November 11. I enclose letter from Felix; it got slit in
opening envelope; forgive. You will note he is very
anxious for you to join them on October 10. For me
I'm afraid I cannot make it. I have to go to Philadelphia
the following week for the Book Fair there; and I don't
think I can make both trips as that weekend I'll be
catching up with my monthly Bk of the Month pressure. But I think you should go anyhow. Write to him
. . . I don't think you need to take globes and beanies;
just the map sections.

I have talked to Harry Scherman and Meredith
Wood, who run the Book of the Month Club, about
the new map. They are genuinely interested in the idea
that it might, eventually, work out as a Book of the
Month Club dividend idea; I told them, of course, that
the whole project was confidential and under consid-
eration by *LIFE*; but they said they'd like to know
more about it.

I suggest you drop a line to Mr Harry Scherman
(he's president of the Bk of the Month Club) at 385
Madison Av and ask him when you could drop in on
him and show him the map. This is a very important
lead.

How'd you like to come out to dinner some evg this
week – maybe Friday? – and have some piano pound-
ing with Bill Colling? Love, haste, Chris.[9]

Bucky replied:

October 7th 42

Dear Christopher:–
All notes and enclosures received – letter herewith
returned. I am off to Haverford Sat. a.m. but <u>sad</u> that
you are not coming – really <u>sad</u>. Now it feels just like
a job – so – you know I understand your not coming
and that I believe in your determination – but that
doesn't stop the fact that to go to Haverford without
you will be a lonelier pilgrimage. And I hardly expect
the savants to be kindly. They rarely are. That is simply
the momentum of Nature.
Very best, Bucky.

P.S. I have deferred calling on Bk of the Month Club
until Life's decision has been made. I will call on them
next Tuesday if no answer from Life by then.[10]

Bucky went to Haverford and the Vector Equilibrium map and
globe had their debut at the opening of 'Government House'.
A photograph of President Morley and R. Buckminster Fuller
together with other speakers appeared in the *Haverford News*
– they were all studying the VE globe. Felix Morley sent Bucky
a warm letter of appreciation with a copy to Chris. Chris sent
his carbon on to Bucky:

Bucky! Felix sent me this carbon – I forward it since I
don't know if 70 Pine St. reaches you. Sorry I had to
run the other day but I was pledged to meet Louise &
her young Scottish officer. Louise is on a plane on her
way to do a job for the State Dept. in England – don't
say the kids don't get around. If you're going out of
town, old horse, try to mail me that old overcoat by
parcel post to Roslyn Hts – I need it for rough work
out here!
Love – Chris[11]

In November 1942 *Thorofare* was published. Bucky wrote:

November 22, 1942

Dear Christopher:–
Up comes the 22 and your book. Have not seen a copy
yet but will get one tomorrow. The reviews as usual
vary all over the lot.
Sounds O.K. to me.
Congratulations.

Affectionately,
Bucky

That's swell news about Louise having an important
overseas flying mission and young Christopher must
be in the midst of that exciting chapter of the war, the
North African mop up, and having taken a continual
part in the bitter early days, of which his heart must be
gladdened.[12]

Chris sent Bucky a copy of *Thorofare* inscribing it 'my own
small contribution to a new Mercator projection'. Geoffrey,
the boy hero of the book, was ten years old when he left
Woodbridge in Suffolk, England, to live in Baltimore, Maryland. The sense of place which Chris always felt strongly was
a fundamental theme in the novel which analysed the minutiae
of Anglo-American differences in order to underline unifying
bonds. *Thorofare* was self-consciously sentimental because
Chris saw his own father in the characterisation of Uncle Dan
and indulged in romanticised reflections about his childhood
memories of England. Chris knew England well thanks to long
trips taken there with his parents during university vacations.
      At Christmas Bucky received an invitation from Chris for
his usual festive get-together. Bucky sent a telegram from
Washington:

CHRISTOPHER MORLEY AND ASSOCIATES
46 WEST 47 (TOP FLOOR) MY ENERGETIC FELLOWSHIP
BY INFINITE FREQUENCY OVER THOUGHT FOCUSSED
BEAM BUCKY[13]

Bucky had gone to Washington to be Chief Mechanical Engineer of the Board of Economic Warfare.

9

Twenty-two Days

In their communications Bucky and Chris frequently referred to the shared pleasures of earlier discussions. The numerological signs seemed extremely favourable when Bucky wrote his first letter to Chris in 1943. He festooned the heading of the Mayflower Hotel notepaper with appropriate calculations:

3422 Garfield St. N. West = 11
Tel Woodley 2900 = 11
BEW Telephone Exec 7030 Branch 2469 = 22

He used so many lines to interconnect his calculations that he remarked:

Looks like Corona Effects were Lurid

Bucky had sent telegrams which he subsequently referred to in a letter as 'cosmograms'.

Thurs Jan 28 '43

Dear Christopher:–
Just a note that should have gone to you with the cosmograms. I hope you will forgive my plagiarism of the Trojan Horse expression – <u>almost</u> 'too bright for <u>their</u> eyes' unconsciously set down by me for I was deeply impressed with that concept of yours. I always

thought it beautiful and amazingly simple and therefore surprising that it had not been said before.
However this use of it sounded well too and may do
some good in helping to condition men's eyes to the
splendour that is all theirs when they learn to contem-
plate their world with some degree of humble adequacy
and daring appreciation of the infinite strength of the
infinitely delicate designing ability of the infinitely
imaginative powers of man.
Affectionately, Bucky[1]

In sharp contrast Chris sent Bucky a valentine:

DR BUCKLING R.U. FULLER
BOARD OF ECONOMIC WARFARE
3422 Garfield St., NW (SPIRAL)
WASHINGTON, D.C.
If not there forward to V.P. Wallace

The picture is of a flying cherub holding a card which says 'I
LOVE YOU'. The hair ribbon is made of two triangular shapes
with Chris labelled HAM and RYE. His sub-caption was FLO into
the FUTURE.[2]

On 1 March 1943, Bucky's map was published in *LIFE*
and the event was suitably celebrated. Chris sent Bucky a
telegram paraphrasing his own 'too bright for my eyes':

LIFE THIS WEEK IS WORTHWHILE COLLYRIUM FOR
MY EYES.[3]

Collyrium was the name of the eyedrops which Chris used
regularly.

Bucky and Allegra had also paid a visit to Roslyn where
they had discussed poetry and Chris had inscribed a copy of
his preface to Bartlett for Allegra. To Bucky he gave a copy of

his *Gutenberg Address*. He kept Bucky supplied with any pieces of his writing which he thought would interest him. The *Gutenberg Address* was a pamphlet he had written the previous year on behalf of the campaign to supply books for the Armed Forces. Back in Washington Bucky wrote:

> *March 4, 1943*
>
> Dear Chris:
> On my return I find your collyrium wire and before leaving New York I received the copy of the speech to the English Association and the Stalingrad poem, all of which I like. Sunday was wonderful and I am sure Allegra feels about it as I do.
> As yours, ever, Bucky[4]

Chris's poem about Stalingrad was called 'The Spoken Word' and written in December 1942. It stressed again the importance in the war of the immediacy of radio and the significance of many voices, accents and place names in the responses we feel:

> *Words are a blessing in the head*
> *Secret to think, difficult to be said,*
> *O spoken word, come clean, Say what you mean,*
> *Be hopeful, humble and exact, servant of fact.*
>
> *For your destiny immense, O spoken words,*
> *   make sense.*
> *However instantaneous you appear,*
> *It's always later There than Here . . .*
> *. . .*
> *Peace will be treated in all sorts of accents –*
> *And Stalingrad? Those best can say it*
> *Who lived in cellars rather than betray it.*[5]

The spoken word would not replace the written one, of course:

> The first stratagem of the Nazis is to destroy books
> which don't agree with them . . . Books are practical
> tools of the spirit . . . God's true country is the human
> mind. Wars are won in the mind before they are won
> in the field. Man, God help him, is the loneliest of crea-
> tures and most lonely in armies. Books are the most
> effective medicine to comfort that hidden sickness. It
> is only in books that man has taken the courage to
> communicate himself without reserve.[6]

The emphasis on shared values as between the British and
the Americans was tremendously important in the war years.
There were those, however, who felt the Anglo-American spiritual bond was exaggerated since there had been so many other
nationalities involved in the development of the United States.
Bucky had prepared a 'Peopling of America' chart which he
loaned to Chris. It showed that the matrix population which
derived from before the American Revolution accounted for
90% of the twentieth-century population. After its return by
Chris, Bucky wrote:

March 8, 1943

Dear Christopher:
Thanks for returning the Peopling of America chart. I
will bet the Great Ammonoosuc and the Little
Ammonoosuc played an important harmonic part in
the spearhead doings of these Northwest spiralling
people, who before us, provided the matrix population,
to which later additions, no matter how diversified, can
be but all spice flavorings, which, though they may
dominate the senses have but little vital contribution
to make in comparison to the vitamin body of the main
broth. Cynthia says this is a little soupy. You will like

Cynthia when you get to see her. I had a delightful note from Dr Morton, who is pleased at the cartographic developments by Corona Effects, Inc., Yours, BF[7] [Cynthia Lacey was Bucky's secretary and ultimately became a member of his company.]

Chris was interested in Bucky's chart because he was at this time developing an idea for a sequel to *Thorofare* which would further emphasise differences between British and American character – but the underlying theme was to be Communication.

As a first generation American with English parents Chris wished to ensure that the people he portrayed in his novel were more fully representative of the traditions of American character than he might be himself. Hence he was undoubtedly glad to discover Bucky's proof that his contemporaries were to a larger degree descended from early British colonists than was generally believed.

Chris was also trying to work into this novel an updated version of Chaucer's allegorical poem *The House of Fame*. Chaucer abandoned the poem and Chris abandoned the novel – probably both for the same reason, the subject matter was too complicated to be presented in the literary form they had chosen.

In the original poem Chaucer described a dream in which he was wafted by an eagle to a great palace placed at an equal distance from earth, sea and sky. Bucky thought of it as a sort of space station. The eagle told Chaucer he would there find stories which he could use. To this spot all sound waves which have ever occurred rippled and were concentrated. Here sat the Goddess of Fame. In his poem 'The Spoken Word' Chris referred to Chaucer's poem:

Not long ago I shot the breeze with Chaucer
(Best friend the English language ever had)

Up to his House of Fame. This he imagined
An over-all control-room or Blue Network,
A listening post for all the talk of men
(To be fully informed read Chaucer every morning),
There are new voices now in the House of Fame
And modes of speech original as Chaucer's
. . .

But Chaucer shames me: 'There's diversite
In English, and in the form of speche is chaunge.'

The poem was at work in Chris's mind while he made his notes
for a continuation of *Thorofare*. He had begun his notes in
September: 'Some preliminary thinking about "*Thorofare*
Extended"' then scribbled over the top 'The House of Fame'.

Vol I leaves Jeff on top of the world.
Vol II should perhaps show what pressures are brought
to bear on him in the period of world explosion. His
only resource, though it takes him a long time to realize
it, is the English language.
. . .

Would it be possible to condense the whole memory
and meaning of the period 1920–1940 into one critical
episode? What was the turning point of the whole era,
when civilisation took the danger-turn?
. . .

Those years 1920–1940 perhaps the saddest the U.S.
ever knew: a half-educated people struggling to begin
to think, or denying what they really knew?
But the behaviourism of those years created intellectual
satire & disgust.
. . .

1933 – shape of Bremen – a warlike shape (although a
passenger ship)
1934 – New Yr modesty (sci mtg) 'Our local galaxy is

94

not the center of supergalaxy'
Feb. 1934 1st saw Dymaxion

Chris's notes described Chaucer's listening post for all the talk of men, quoting partly from Chaucer and partly writing in his own words:

> *The palace of magnifying beryl*
> *The great gate carved 'by aventure wrought as often*
>   *as by care'*
> *come the attendants, asking handouts,*
> *wearing innumerable coat-armours (emblems)*
> *then the changeable (ebb and flow) femynine creature*
> *many eyes, ears, tongues*
> *making her decisions capriciously*
> *& calls for Aeolus the god of wind to blow his*
>   *two trumpets*
> *Clear Laud (gold) and slander (black).*

Chaucer was present while the capricious goddess, all tongues, eyes and ears, decided whose fame would be proclaimed by Aeolus with the gold trumpet of praise and whose as scandal, with black. Attendants approached him for money to sing his praises but he quickly told them he was there to observe. He was staggered to discover there was no logic in Fame's decisions – she was completely capricious. An attendant then conducted him to an establishment made of woven reeds rather like a beehive in which there was a great humming and buzzing while people told things to each other and there was no way of knowing whether what escaped through the gaps was true or false.

Chaucer had now reached the limits of his fancy and broke off with the statement 'There then came a Man of Great Authority . . .' and that was where he finished. Some think the ending deliberate, cut off sharply as dreams often end. It is possible he intended a comparison between the traditions of classical mythology and the later Christian ethic.

Chris intended to use the House of Fame to symbolise an advertising agency or a radio network and the capricious goddess was the great power of telecommunication. He recognised the influence of 'the Media' on our social habits and our choices. In his own handwriting at the side of the page of typed notes he wrote:

Freedom of the press is freedom to exercise judgement.[8]

Chris began work on the early chapters of *The House of Fame* using a character from upstate New York who appeared in the original novel of *Thorofare*. He intended that this manufacturer should meet once again Jeff [i.e. Geoffrey when grown up], the hero of *Thorofare*, and get him involved in advertising and journalism. Unfortunately Chris became bogged down in a long and complicated description of a train journey to the opening of Grand Central Station and he never continued the book.

Chris certainly intended to locate some of the action in this novel in Schenectady. He went there with Bucky in 1943 and at the request of a book collector they autographed a copy of the presentation book about the New York World's Fair together – Bucky making a sketch of the evolution of the Dymaxion theory close to where Chris spoke of 'a new slope for right-angles ideas'.[9]

During the trip to Schenectady in May 1943 the roles of the two men were reversed. It was Bucky who had a professional reason for going and Chris went along, although he did not have a public engagement. Bucky's responsibilities at the Board of Economic Warfare concerned geopolitical aspects of the war effort. His experience with problems connected with his map projection provided the necessary experience for an assignment which he undertook shortly after his arrival in Washington. He explained:

To understand our letters you have to know the background.

At that time in the war Churchill's grand strategy was to attack the 'soft belly' of Europe. We were to try to get into Italy from North Africa. This meant radio-controlled bombing, and that meant a continuous triangulation survey of the Earth's surface from the U.S.A. to North Africa was crucial, not only to planning but to the triangulated radio directional control of bombing missions. By 1943 the U.S. continental triangulation grid had reached the Texas-Mexico border. But when Churchill introduced his plan it meant that the triangulation had to be taken southward through Mexico and Central America and then eastward through Brazil and across the South Atlantic to North Africa, then northward across the Mediterranean to Sicily and to Europe. The U.S.A. had to get this grid.

In exchange for Brazilian cooperation, Bucky added, President Vargas wanted a five year plan for the economic development of his country, similar to the Russian Five Year Plan. Bucky was responsible for the preparatory work connected with this and travelled round to interview some of the American engineers who had been to Russia. Schenectady was the first city he visited.[10]

After their return Chris wrote to Anne:

May 24 1943

Dear Anne,

I'm very much ashamed, I forgot I was still wearing Bucky's cuff links. I'm afraid if I send them after him they won't catch him, so I'm mailing them to 105 East 88 under separate cover.

The little trip to Schy was highly instructive.

Love to you all, Chris[11]

Bucky worked very swiftly on his plan, as indeed the experts did on the triangulation. In July Chris wrote to Bucky for his birthday and mentioned the first bombing raid on Sicily:

R.B.F.

July 12 MCXLIII

Noble Buckling: they pretty nearly chose yr birthday to start the Sicilian Vespers – only this morning I said to myself: This is a Special Day, what is't? Flag Day? Steuben Day? New England Boiled Dinner Day? The Feast of Saint Humid? The anniversary of the Battle of the Boyne (By God I think it is: Orangemen's Day? The day Pop Foyle always drank Vat 69)

To me chiefly, it is the Day after the Wedding Day of my Father and Mother who were united in matrimony at St Peter's in the East, Oxford, July 11, 1889 – But ever since yr message so full of Pathos – 'I'm wishing myself Happy Birthday from you' – well Wini reminded me, and Here I am, old Decatur, and a bundle of affte [affectionate] considerations from Chris

P.S. Your birthday present is the excessively rare Polish 5c stamp on the envelope – See to it.[12]

Wini was Elizabeth Winspear, Chris's secretary for many years, who helped him with all aspects of his work. Letters she typed were always identified with cm/ebw. Chris's letter is stylishly decorated by him with pointing fingers and embellished capitals. In his 'considerations' there is a reminder of Ammonoosuc. With his reply to Chris, Bucky sent a copy of his confidential document on the plan for Brazil:

July 16, 1943

Dear Christopher,
I am delighted with my birthday present. I asked

Cynthia to read it out loud to me, nice and slowly so that we could have more time for the fun. It certainly was a wonderful trip and the story seems to be written just as if it is happening all over again. How wonderful the atmosphere was that afternoon – one of those rare clear days which become golden as it grows. We are going to have to open up some even longer stretches of the Northwest passage together. We may even have to take the swing along its Southern Hemisphere counter-part, sprung suddenly as a refrigerated offshoot of the main stem. I also loved having the birthday letter, itself, which arrived on the twelfth – not this time as a self-addressed returned greeting.

One should really give presents on one's birthday. I am therefore sending you enclosed (for your confi-dential perusal) a copy of the tentative outline accruing to the trip of investigation, whose starting leg to Schenectady you paced.

If you can make another trip down here, don't forget that I now have a house and room for you any time (at 2222 Decatur Place N.W., Washington, D.C.) Despite the cataclysmic changes announced today in the paper regarding the auspices of economic warfaring we are still on active duty in that method of engage-ment of the enemy.

Affectionately,

B.F.

P.S. Hello and special regards from Cynthia.[13]

Postal Zone 19

July 23, 1943

Good Old Buckling,

The tentative report on Brazil is of most extraordinary interest . . . Of course there is and always will be the difficulty of swinging the bridge of San Luis Rey between the gorgeous vision of what devoted effort could make out of green hell, and the solid pragmatist (Tory if you will) who cannot believe state planning and free enterprise may consort together. I guess that handsome concessions will have to be made on both sides? As a sparkplug or essay in ignition I find your Brazilian report one of the most inflammable and exciting things you have ever done. It starts notions which immediately begin to fizz and fume in all directions. Naturally I am particularly curious about page 4 which has been carefully excised from the copy you sent me. I groan a little here and there at the highly personal prose you employ for exposition. I always enjoy it, but sometimes fear it may retard some students.

If you have any available extra copies I can't help wishing you would try one on William McFee, Brookfield, Conn. Mac, as a long-trained engineer and a keen observer of Latin American habits would be particularly interested. It seems to me you have attacked the fundamental issues (geography, climate, airborne trend, natural resources, & c) with your shrewdest facility. Admitting instantly the vast difficulties in the way, and wondering also whether Brazilian statesmanship – or any other statesmanship – is yet adequate to your wise purview, I do believe you have broken fresh ground and fresh air in an essay of geo-economy which will be long remembered. I want very much to hear you talk about all this. Meanwhile this is just an exclamation of strong pleasure. I most want to hear what the Brazilian commentators will say. It was sagacious to remind their proud spirits that to invite an outside expert is not a humiliation.

Affectionately,

Chris

cm:ebw

P.S. 1. Make the most of this beautiful letter because for a while anything due from me won't be nearly so perfect: Wini goes into the WAVES next week. [The WAVES were the US Navy's Women's Auxiliary.]

P.S. 2. In re State Planning vs. Free Enterprise remember your old Kipling 'It is not learning, grace nor gear, nor easy meat and drink, But bitter pinch of pain and fear that makes creation think.'[14]

What Bucky had proposed was a plan for Brazil which would use the new triangulation grid to plot landing strips five hundred miles apart, 'criss-crossing Brazil's ten million square miles of Green Hell' which was impenetrable to road and rail access but could be developed by the use of air transport. He further explained:

It is interesting that at the time of my report, Brazil, contrary to popular U.S. conceptioning, was already committed by necessity exclusively to an air transport plan, and in 1944 had more licensed air pilots than had the U.S.A. and was flying its farmers, hens, chickens and cows about by airplanes as an everyday pattern analogous to U.S.A. farm trucking over country roads and highways. Although my plan was very compatible to Brazil it didn't have much chance of being put immediately into comprehensive effect. I also sent the plan to top private people like Chris to get their reactions which is why he mentioned the various aspects which excited him.[15]

Energetic Geometry

Apart from work for the Board of Economic Warfare, Bucky's main concern at this time was public reaction to the map and Chris continued to be extremely interested as well.

March 18, 1943

Dear Christopher:

Thanks for the pamphlet on Scripta Mathematica activities and publications. This is rich in the kind of reference material that most intrigues me. I looked at the item in the *Times* regarding the butterfly map. You might be interested in the enclosed carbon of a reply I have written to someone else on the same subject, as well as a carbon of a letter written to a kinsprit cartographer who had written some kind remarks about the Dymaxion projection . . . The many letters received by *LIFE* promise large educational development for the map. The next two issues of *LIFE's* Letters to the Editor will have some amusing items regarding the map.

Spring is here in Washington. Has it arrived in the Knot Hole today? Isn't it time to call a meeting of the Committee to Do Something about Spring?

R. Buckminster Fuller

Economic Trench Digger

Economic Task Force in the Cosmic Theatre of Operations[1]

Later that year Chris drew Bucky's attention to another map projection which was being widely publicised. The rival map used an icosahedron. In a three-page letter to Chris, Bucky elaborated on the difference stating that the 'icosahedron' was not an 'invention'. This form of polygon was well known to the Greeks. Bucky had decided not to use it for his world map because it had three degrees more distortion than the Vector Equilibrium, 63 vs 60, and the icosahedron's twenty tetrahedras' interior vertices did not coincide with the centre of the sphere and therefore were not subject to symmetrical great circle grid subdivision as was only the Vector Equilibrium. He concluded:

It must be remembered that a new method of projection doesn't happen every day. The Dymaxion method constitutes actually true invention in the jurisprudential sense of the word. In every known projection except the Dymaxion, all error is centrifugally disposed from a center line or arc towards the outer area of the surface to which the projection is made. The Dymaxion is true throughout its enclosing boundary and adjusts the reduction of the spherical to the plane surface towards the center. Because radiant area increases outwardly as the square of the radius, error corrected outwardly as against error inwardly is accomplished only by proportions of error in square magnitudes on a three to one basis in all methods of projection other than the Dymaxion. I'm ready to prove mathematically that angular error and proportional area are subjected to less deformation in the Dymaxion than in any other known mathematical method of translating spherical data as plane surface data.

Coronas resplendent,
Bucky[2]

This further exchange of letters about the map came towards the end of the year, twelve months after the first public showing at Haverford. Chris had been trying to set up a visit for himself to Bucky but when this fell through he still drew Bucky's attention to an article he had noticed:

Be sure in your reference library at B.E.W. to look up the October issue of Geographical Review (of the American Geographic Society) which contains article by I. Fisher on his Icosahedral Globe (with reference to the Dymaxion Globe) and also an article by yr friend Rick Harrison – Love to you all – Chris[3]

Later, in 1954, Bucky decided to use the icosahedron himself. He explained:

The Vector Equilibrium gave minimum distortion but people didn't like it because it was much easier for them to understand the icosa with twenty faces which were all processed exactly by the same projection transformation.

Although all the edge lengths of the VE were the same with uniformly 60 degrees of arc, people just couldn't accept the VE triangular and square faces as being equally projected. So to eliminate further objection I used the icosa, which is the VE symmetrically contracted with a little larger edge arc, 63.26 degrees.

When LIFE had decided to go ahead with my map in 1943 their art editor insisted on orienting it as exactly symmetrical around the north-south polar axis. My friend Ricky Harrison was given the task of producing the cartographic work and he did not understand that I had discovered a new mathematical method of projection from a sphere to a planar surface. He used a conventional mathematical shadow projection method which produced a non-uniform boundary scale along the edges of the square and triangular faces of the VE and this is the way my *LIFE* edition was published. His method shrunk the land masses more than the ocean areas. Just as the *LIFE* publication of my map was coming off the presses Ricky Harrison told me he had had a telephone call from Professor Fisher at Yale asking him to do a similar projection to the one he'd done for me but on an icosahedron and this was published a few months later by *LIFE*'s competitor *Look* Magazine. A year earlier when *LIFE*'s editors were considering the publication of my map, they asked a number of experts about it to ensure that it was an entirely original idea. The experts stated it was 'pure invention' using the phrase in a derogatory sense since it didn't conform with any then known mathematical method. Later this did me a good turn since producing these letters persuaded the Patent Office to reconsider my application for a cartographic patent after a 1900 U.S. patent examiner's decision that no cartographic patents would be granted as all possible mathematical methods had been invented. So in 1946 I was allowed Patent number 2,393,676. Chris was always thrilled about my map and everything to do with it. It was the same with the dome later on . . .

. . . Imagine how excited Chris would have been to find the 90th meridian going right through the floor of the dome I designed for a religious center at Carbondale for Southern Illinois University.[4]

Both Bucky and Chris liked to think that there was a cosmic significance in coincidences like this – the fact that Bucky should be asked to design a dome which would be located on the meridian which he had intuitively used for his first north/south map – for the end-papers for *Nine Chains to the*

Moon, and the basis of a model produced for Bucky by Bill Baird.

In 1943 Chris's appearances on the radio programme *Information Please* made him an even more widely known public figure. As a result he found he had to barricade himself against interruptions in the time he set apart for writing or reading preparatory to Book-of-the-Month meetings. He was still pleased to join in the convivial activities but only if the timing suited him. In addition to his own family responsibilities he had a family from Scotland as his guests for the duration of the war. They lived in the house he had bought to accommodate war evacuees. In Roslyn he helped with the community victory garden, and jokingly referred to it as the Roslyn Soviet of Vegetable Producers in order to create the initials RSVP. He became Commissar of Beets and Eggplant.

After Wini went into the WAVES Chris personally typed a good deal of his own correspondence, keeping carbons of business letters. Most of the letters to Bucky were personally typed.

Towards the end of 1943 Bucky's mind was turning again towards housing, with a view to postwar developments. Improved technology in the aircraft industry would, he felt, make it possible to mass produce housing on a hitherto unprecedented scale. Serving now with the Foreign Economic Administration he had responsibility for thinking ahead to the replacement of housing in Europe destroyed by war. Early in 1944 Bucky circulated copies of a number of letters he had written in which he analysed and considered the possibilities of converting the aircraft industry to peacetime production, and he wrote to Chris:

February 12, 1944

Dear Chris,
Here is the latest vintage of our Dymaxion thinking. I have been receiving encouraging results from the effort which is documented in it. The items describe the

conversion of certain major areas of the war production ability to the mass production of components for
a scientific dwelling machine service industry. They
refer particularly to the suppliers of materials and
component parts for the aircraft parts. This conversion
program would not be thought of as a panacea. It is
true that it has satisfied many obvious requirements.
This in itself should not make us sceptical. Rather it
should be thought of as one plan not only we but
anyone can see 'will work'. It is not what new materials
will substitute in obsolete mechanics, it is what
comprises the whole family of new mechanics which
will make obsolete the old troubles; not a further array
of unrelated plastic gadgets, but a new comprehensive
industry, vast, yet excitingly personal.
Sincerely yours,
Bucky
P.S. [In Bucky's handwriting] On two flying trips to
N.Y.C. recently I tried to telephone you but find service
discontinued. Where are you?[5]

Later Bucky explained:

The original Dymaxion House was designed with a
view to being produced by the aircraft industry. It was
designed to be manufactured with the highest technology and capability and the most high performance
materials and chemical elements which went into
weaponry: into aircraft, armament and battleships. I
wanted to take these capabilities and apply them to the
home front to take care of human beings . . .

In this letter what I was saying was that we were
getting nearer to the time when the 1927 house might
be realisable. Originally I said fifty years. The Dymaxion Deployment Unit was one phase in its evolution.

That's why in the drawing I did for the autograph in Schenectady I showed the DDU growing into the Dymaxion House.[6]

Chris did not reply to this letter with all its enclosures. A few weeks later Bucky wrote again:

March 21, 1944

Dear Chris,
Here is a copy of the *Energetic Geometry* disclosure.

It was prepared especially for copyrighting the elements of proof – tables, constructions etc. Instruction was not required and therefore not attempted. Explanation will probably be made in a regular edition of one of the larger publications in the near future. I thought you might be interested in having this early item for your records.
Sincerely yours,
Bucky[7]

Bucky explained:

The reason for this was to establish my copyright. I found out from the Library of Congress what the copyright laws were and was told if I printed and sent more than two hundred copies of my ideas and sent them interstate and had proof of doing so I could get it copyrighted. I produced 240 copies and sent each out by registered mail and got the receipts back. I fastened them to the list of those to whom I had sent it. That got me both the copyright and a scientifically satisfactory date of 'publishing'.[8]

During Bucky's time in Washington he was a member of a group of scientists who met at the Cosmos Club. Many of them were working on secret projects which were classified. Discussions were informal but Bucky was advised by one of the British scientists that some of his ideas might relate to the regularities in electron shells around atoms which were then only slowly being understood. In the circumstances he thought Bucky ought to publish.

Bucky's *Energetic Geometry* was the beginning of his *Synergetic Geometry*; he felt that his statement 'Unity is plural and at minimum two' was tremendously important because the Vector Equilibrium was related to the structural pattern of the universe. For the outward and inwards forces of the VE to be exactly balanced they had to counteract each other. So unity must involve two forces, positive and negative. When packing spheres of equal size into the tightest possible arrangement around a central sphere, the number of spheres in the outermost layer always coincided with an exact formula – ten times the number of layers squared plus two. After 92 (the number of pure natural elements) the systems invariably interacted but the formula nevertheless remained correct.

$$12 = 10 + 2 \left(10 \times 1^2 + 2\right)$$
$$42 = 40 + 2 \left(10 \times 2^2 + 2\right)$$
$$92 = 90 + 2 \left(10 \times 3^2 + 2\right)$$
$$162 \text{ etc.}$$

Chris had been incommunicado for some time but *Energetic Geometry* roused him.

22 March, 1944

Good and patient Buckling!
I got your letters and most interesting documents; I plead guilty. I no longer have the inspiration of Wini to dictate to. I've been dilly dallying along with some intricate work and about the time yr last arrived I was very low in a grippe that hung on for a long time. Just

briefly I was in too wretched spirits to write a decent letter. And the bloody old Bk of the Month Club has been practically a full time job if one did nothing else. But I can't let this new 22 day of a twice 22 year go by without sending you my love. I was thinking only last night of how we celebrated my crossing of the shadow line of Life Expectancy – July 28, 1938, I think it was – jesusgod one has had going on 6 years of actuarial velvet since then. Have you reckoned up when yr own Shadow Line will arrive? We should celebrate it in some mercurial ritual; 9 chains to Utopia or whatever; I assume that by yr birth date you have a slightly longer expectation than I had. Mine was, if I remember 48.23 years, and by God and Thank God how I fooled the tables.

The only retaliation I can send you is enclosed. Sherlock Holmes' Prayer! Not as impt as Energetic Geometry – please send a copy of letter to my bro FVM whose office is Room 5329, Dept of Labor Bldg Washn D.C. – he is now a full time member of the War Labor Board & has been doing a champion job: he sent me copies of his recent speeches, in Denver and in Youngstown, Ohio (Sheet and Tube city!). They are really superb. He is temperamentally a true statesman. This is brief because I'm on my way down to the Institute for the Blind, I'm doing three days work there this week, reading onto records for the blind some of the Sherlock Holmes stories that have never been done that way before. I was really tickled. The last person who read Holmes-Watson for them was Colin Keith Johnston, and they told me that they thought I put more character into the reading than he did. The old frustrated ham again.

God Bless. I look forward with some horror to going back to L.I. a month hence where I suppose I'll have to swink and wamble once more in victory gardening. [Chris had taken an apartment in New York City for several months to simplify domestic arrangements.]

Don't be chagrined in silence; it mostly means the honest attempt to work. Always yr devoted Chris[9]

Bucky's reply:

April 6, 1944

Dear Chris,
My spirits rose 40,000 feet upon receipt of your letter. For whatever good it may do us, we are still in the stratosphere. Come and see us some time.
Affectionately, Bucky[10]

One might wonder what link there was between *Energetic Geometry* and the prayer which Chris wrote for the Baker Street Irregulars' dinner in March 1944, which began:

Grant me, O spirit of Reason, matter for Deduction, Intuition, and Analysis . . .
. . . (and Section 4)
If in hours of dullness neither the Turkish bath nor medieval charters, nor my scrapbooks, nor my fiddle avail to soothe, turn my attention to the infallible reactions of chemistry or to that rational and edifying insect the Bee.[11]

When Conan Doyle was finally allowed by his reading public to let Sherlock Holmes retire, the activity chosen for the detective was bee-keeping. The connection between Bucky's earlier theories and his new ideas was quite clear to Chris. Bucky never became a Baker Street Irregular although he had enjoyed conversations with Vincent Starrett about Penang lawyers and many occasions with Bill Hall, another of Chris's close friends, who was an active participant.

The Sherlock Holmes activities developed into an organisation which continues to this day and provided enjoyable recreation then as now. During the spring of 1944, however, Chris was hoping that something more important would come along to occupy his mind. He was hoping for an overseas posting.

11

Self-Searching Toulemonde

In May of 1944 Bucky telephoned to Chris in a moment of crisis. This prompted Chris to send him the typescript carbon of one of his recent poems:

May 19, 1944

My old and notable Buckling!
I was happy to have your call.
My mind is very busy. Here is something (printed a few weeks ago in the Sat. Review), that may amuse you. I was tickled that my ever-blessed W, (Wini) ran into you the very day she was sending me a bday present. God bless! CM

The poem was 'Toulemonde Intermezzo'. Bucky marked one passage:

I had my eras one by one;
Each was dear, each had its fun,
But man must learn, or his name is mud,
To relish the ebb as well as the flood.
Even In all this woe, we guess
Are growing pains for the U.S.
Global citizen began it
When men-about-town became Men-about-planet.
Just now in partisan catalepse

Rather wavering are our steps
But all depends on the will-to-think –
Steward! Did you forget that drink?
Plain water, if you please; not Schweppes.

Oh lovely lonely lucid hours
When thought swings up to its full powers,
When ego, fantailed like a peacock
Can find the needle in the haycock
And hold the needle's eye and thread it –
Is that millennium? You said it![1]

Bucky replied:

May 22, 1944

Dear Christopher:

Happy 22 of May day!

The middle-aged poet sounds like a snorting stallion kicking up the daisies in the meadows and making the spring sweet-stink even more richly of everything. Your poem made me think of an amazing though gradual experience of my own which has grown out of an original desire to give everything important away. When I first started Dymaxion research, I used to say that for every invention freely released to anyone trying to take it away from me (and it had to happen that they did the trying) I was refreshed with two new inventions. That was just the beginning. I went on to realization of the existence of an infinite number of surprise keys to the great reality.

After I had opened this door and that door, each one of which had seemed the only door of the moment through into great wonderment, and after I had given the key to the door to someone else, many times I suddenly began to see the doors from above me as so many foundations with walls and roofs long since gone but the doorways still agape, all dotted here and there. And standing in line around these foundations, great numbers of people are still groping. For my own humble self, as must many before me, I have come to realize that there are no doors. It is all real inside and out.

I think the wonderful feeling one has with ships and the sea – or just with the boats and the waters (a feeling you and I shared when we were flying together) is of going from here to there without having to go in or through doors. It is a naked extension of reality to include all the personally discovered places and events as a wonderful continuity. It is amazing how the myriad of egoes themselves have been confused by the change in inward or outward emphasis of the greatest cosmic conceptioning of man, in his moments of lucid scientific reasoning. The individual has wheeled and swung like the tiniest bird in great flight in the largest cosmological patterns, singing 'Yes, we have no bananas' as he does his bit in the extravaganza 'Expanding universe'. And anyway what you say now is right, as right as any human word can be – and that is that the inward and outward struggle of man is for the moment deprived of equilibrious fulfilment pending his demonstration of the will to think. As homo sapiens, he has come of age in full realization of his faculties and facilities. He has thoroughly affirmed his materialism; he must affirm his appreciative faculties. So God bless the O.M.

The more you try to disengage gracefully and unselfishly from the preoccupation of the stage of living delight, the more you will find the play moving off or upstage with you. You only bring life into increasing focus by trying to unburden it of your limitations.

Nothing fertilises vitality as well as a cast off coat of personal inertias and priorities. You can take an Old Castle on a hill for granted. It will still be there tomorrow without man's continuing efforts; but you can't take an airplane in flight for granted. She has to be constantly flown and her dynamic parts and functioning must be continually checked over. I prefer life that way, even though an airplane can crash and a castle cannot.

[In his own handwriting Bucky added:]

Am off for a week at Sea Island, Georgia, 'The Cloisters' to shake off the shingles. Many thanks for your prompt and effective reply to my cry of pain. Affectionately, BF[2]

In July Chris sent Bucky a long birthday letter to bring him up to date:

10 July, 1944

Noble Buckling:–

This is your birthday letter! The 12th July, you may remember was also the date old Pop Foyle always celebrated by wearing an Orange sash and getting himself a bit pied.

The weather is such that a tall cold drink is a great temptation; but I don't dare take one. I've got to go to town presently for an Info Please program, so I'm sitting here with a glass of iced tea. The thermometer just outside the window, in the sun, says 102 (it's 4 p.m.) The readings at the same time, the last four days have been 104, 105, 103, 102 – which corresponds to about a steady 90 in the shade on the other side of the house. I have to smile a little at poor old de Gaulle who probably imagined when he left Africa that he'd get some coolth. But I reckon nobody in Washn wants to be reminded of the heat. I talked to my bro Frank a few minutes ago, he has a rigid stiff neck from going between air-conditioned Labor office and Washington streets and has to have it massaged by osteopath. I have also talked to bro Felix who is in town today – he and I are going to have a plate of something at Billy Oyster-man's before the Info Please – he says that after the GOP convention in Chicago nothing will ever seem hot to him again. By the way I thought your friend Claire Luce's speech was dreadful. The mere fact that she would quote Archbp Spellman under the notion that is poetry is gall to my spook. The poet I have resorted to lately, in moments of groping, is E.E. Cummings, who has a really beautiful mind. In spite of sweat and a sore arm from vaccination I think my best hours lately have been on all fours in the community garden weeding beets etc. in blazing sun. There's a kind of reality that tickles the soul every time you rescue a young infant beet from the crowing parasites – and now the Jap beetles are on us again; just when we'd recovered from a beating given by the inchworms.

I have just got (from a 2nd hand bookseller in Newton Center, Mass) a cheap copy of *The Martyr-dom of Man*, the wonderful book so highly praised by Sherlock Holmes. I had a copy years ago but it got away from me somehow; then I found one which I gave to Edgar Smith; now by God I have one for myself again. The title is grimly appropriate to these days. Of course when he published the book (1872) his denial of anthropomorphic God and his insistence that 'immortality' was only a charming illusion, were pretty sour doctrine to most of his readers. But one can still admire the excellent words of his preface – and adapt them to whatever personal heresies are needed today:-

'My conscience is my adviser, my audience, and my

judge. It bade me write as I have written, without evasion, without disguise. If my religious opinions should be condemned without a single exception, by every reader of the book, it will not make me regret having expressed them, and it will not prevent me from expressing them again . . . It has done me good to write this book: and therefore I do not think it can injure those by whom it will be read.'

I had thought that this very week I would be away, high, wide and handsome (?) on the wings of aircraft; and I got myself dosed with typhoid and smallpox per instructions; but the projected doings have not been okayed in Washn and I reckon that while the flying bomb business is so bad the govts simply (and quite understandably) don't want unnecessary civilians floating about. Letters from Louise arrived today, written only 8 days ago, suggest between the lines that the experience is pretty damnable. Whether it is London, or Saipan, Saseby or Vilna, the martyrdom of man proceeds apace. The village of La Haye du Puits just captured by the U.S. Army was one I used to bicycle to in 1924. The BBC have just offered me ½ hour of radio time to talk to British audience, to tell them anything about USA that one thinks the English would be interested in. What would you say? Pretty damn hard to speak from so far behind the lines to people who have gone through hell's thick of it??? Would you say anything? Chris is also in England but I don't know where. He seems to be in some camp in a very restricted area. I suppose there'll be another invasion soon – how else can they halt the damn robots. Can't you devise some neutralising curtain of electrical antibodies that wd take the starch out of the damned things?

I was very greatly pleased by a story from Copenhagen about some Danes who wanted to do some 'non-explosive' sabotage, viz get the citizens whistling or singing tunes offensive to the Nazis – so they set up a phonograph on a rooftop and when the Danes were all coming out of a big movie house got them humming *Lillibulero*, an old 18th century soldier song little known here, but very familiar in Europe. In fact it's the tune the pirates always whistled in *Treasure Island*; it's still the theme song of some BBC European broadcast.

Now I must take a bath & change clothes & catch 5 pm train to town: an hour's work at the office and then check up with Dan Golenpaul.

Blessings and all happiest returns, old splitter of atoms.

Chris[3]

Chris was bitterly disappointed later not to be able to go on the overseas mission which he mentioned in this letter. The authorities refused permission on medical grounds. The problem was high blood pressure. His fears about the possibility of a stroke like Don Marquis's were re-aroused. Chris became morbidly preoccupied about his health. How worried he was can be deduced from a later comment in *The Man Who Made Friends with Himself* when his hero said:

> Going past the news-stand I feel a blood pressure. The least prick of pain horrifies me, instantly I struggle to rationalise. Partake of the competitive spirit up to the point where its comedy (or tragedy) becomes personally noticeable. Then retire at once as a wellbred verb to the perfect passive participle . . . Hurrying upstairs is always a spiritual tizzy because the doctor told me it might be fatal.[4]

Bucky in the meantime was considering plans which subsequently took him to Wichita to work directly on his scheme for a new industry. He marked the occasions when he crossed the Mississippi by sending postcards to Chris:

August 15, 1944

Once more across the Mississippi
Corona Effects vivid.

October 22, 1944

Here we go over the Mississippi again, outward bound Oct. 22 (by no contrivance of my own in company with 4 directors of Dymaxion Dwelling Machines, Inc. after its first board meeting (also 22 Oct to conference prototyping in Wichita of First Dwelling Machine (100%) (Over the River 4.55 a.m.) A serious Task Ahead but with much good will. B.F.[5]

After the new company was launched Bucky sent Chris progress reports on all the developments. Chris reciprocated with news of his own activities:

February 6 – '45

Noble Buckling – Certainly yr Industrial Strategy Map puts you at the very Node of Nodes – or Inganglion of Ganglia or Navel of the Continent, the very Nombril as Chaucer wd call it of Numerology. Like yourself I've been and continue busy, though I can't point to much achievement – except, by God (now I think of it!) a poem I'll enclose to you which I shall publish one of these days! Much love from Chris.[6]

The poem was 'Ballad of New York, New York'. The type-script was headed '(Not for publication – am still tinkering with it – but I'd love to know how you like it, read aloud!) Chris.'
Bucky replied:

February 24, 1945

Dear Chris:

I like 'New York, New York'. Now acquiring the perspective of Wichita upon the Empire State I find a number of references fading into obscurity, such as Harbor Hill and bullgine 33. Yet as a Wichitan I would like to enjoy 'New York, New York' and as such would believe that one per cent of the words trip me up in enjoying the 99 per cent that synchronises with the universal mind. I just say this because, as you say, you are still tinkering with it. There are some really wonderful spots in it. I'll take that crosstown street!

Affectionately,

Bucky

Hello! Cynthia[7]

In a later and published version of the poem 'bullgine' became Number 33:

Around the bend of Harbor Hill
Comes Number 33
Says: Board the cars, my bonny boy,
And ride to Town with me.[8]

There were no less than five versions of the poem before Chris was entirely satisfied and had incorporated suggestions from various people with which he agreed. The most important (handwritten) document of this phase of the correspondence is from Bucky:

July 12, 1945

CHRISTOPHER

B. FULLER IS 50

Not 50/50

JUST 50

AND

THE MAINMAST (BURNISHED STAINLESS STEEL) AND
MAIN STRUCTURAL CAGE OF THE FIRST GENUINE
DYMAXION HOUSE WERE ASSEMBLED FOR THE FIRST
TIME JULY 9 COMMENCING AT 2.30 P.M. CENTRAL WAR
TIME AND COMPLETING AT 4.30 P.M. ON THE SAME
DAY JUST EIGHTEEN YEARS FROM CONCEPTION.
THANKS GOD.[9]

Bucky had not yet abandoned a central mast as a feature of
his design for the Dymaxion house. The dome was still to
come.

During the rest of the summer and autumn of 1945 there
was a gap in the correspondence. Chris had started work on
another edition of *Bartlett's Familiar Quotations*. Helen Hare
and Bob Levitt were assisting him in his New York office. He
obviously wrote to Bucky (untraced letter) suggesting that
Bucky let him have a quote to include. Bucky replied (another
handwritten letter):

> *December 14, '45*
>
> Christopher:–
> I will be in N.Y. for Christmas!
> Your letter gave me a terrific lift. Am harnessing a team
> of high powered lit'ry horses for Bartlett's table.
> Enclosed a new Dymaxion item.
> Love Bucky[10]

It took some time for Bucky to send all the material in which
he thought Chris would be particularly interested for Bartlett.
In January Chris sent him a packet of matches from a department store in Wichita that turned up in his study, suggesting
Bucky visit it and give them his love. Bucky replied some weeks
later:

March 6, 1946

Dear Chris:

Innes's is very much in the heart of Wichita – and is our No. 1 merchandising emporium. I will attempt to establish myself with them via the match safe. I am enclosing news items and copy of my cartographic patent. I believe it to be the first projection to be granted a United States patent. I thought you might like it signed for your Dymaxiana.

I will be in New York approximately March 14, 1946. Fuller Houses Incorporated is to be introduced to the press on March 21. This means a 22 day public release. (I promise you I did not arrange that.) Our staff now counts 65 members and much goes on beyond my ken.

I asked a young man, Sonny Applewhite, recently a Lt. Commander in the Navy and now my personal editor to pick out some Dymaxion quotes to submit to you. I am enclosing a few preliminary items. These are all from a new book we are printing out here for the company. I will send you a copy when it comes off the press (titled 'Designing a New Industry'). This was a recording I gave to our engineering staff here. Our engineering staff comprises 30 lead aeronautical engineers culled from Boeing, Curtiss-Wright, Bell, Globe and Beech companies etc. As I write I have been handed an organization chart of Fuller Houses Incorporated so will slip it in too. I don't remember if I sent you one of the Dymaxion Dwelling Machine calling cards, so I am also throwing that into this Morley packet.
Love, Bucky[11]

In April Bucky sent Chris postcards from Colorado where he was having a vacation. At the end of the month Chris replied to the various communications:

April 30, 1946

Bucky:

Today rediscovered memo of your quotations – put them in my bag. Engine of Train, Number 22. Number of car I rode in Number 1894. 'What do you think of that, my dog?' Been working very hard I feel like Euclid's cubic block – deprived of time element.

Who do you suppose is typing this? I will let her explain.

Love,

Bucky Dear, as Mr Churchill would say, 'It's me – Helen Hare Carroll, thinking fondly of nine chains to new London and Fairfield. Cheerio!'[12]

The reference to Euclid's cubic block being deprived of the time element harked back to a comment made by Bucky in *Nine Chains to the Moon*. Bucky's next letter followed quickly:

May 10, 1946

Dear Chris:

Here are two items:

1. 'Bucky Fuller's Notebook' A Close up of B.F. for *Life* by Russell Davenport (never published) written 1943.
2. 'Designing a New Industry' by B.F. as yet unpublished item in collated form – to be distributed sometime – I believe. These contain many quotes and I thought you might consider some one or two for the Bartlett's edition. I wonder how 'Designing a New Industry' might do for a Book of the Month dividend item – as the subject is now broadly popular. Would you like to have additional copies? The type is set here in Wichita at McCormick Armstrong's.

Love,

Bucky[13]

It was odd that from all this material Chris chose a quotation from Bucky's poem 'No More Secondhand God'.

While he was in Wichita, Bucky learned to fly, passed tests for a pilot's license and began to fly his own plane. Early in 1947, Bucky wrote to Chris a long excited letter in his own handwriting:

3/3/47

Dear Christopher:

Thought you might enjoy the enclosed. Here is my Luscombe. I passed my test for my private pilot certificate in December. I swiftly flew to Chicago from Wichita for $6.00 thence to Cleveland, and Columbus, Indianapolis, St Louis, Kansas City and return to Wichita in 20 hours total flying time Wichita to Wichita and for a grand total 1800 miles at 100 gals of gas and 3 quarts of oil costing $22.00. Hangar fees at various airports for 2 weeks cost an average of $1.00 per day or $14.00. I made a speaking tour and the net was good after all expenses in hotels etc. I know you would be thrilled at my flying my own plane over the Mississippi. Note that the right hand side of the radio beam passes right over Navour, Ill. I have traced in red pencil the route which I remember as being that of the wonderful motor trip with the Ralph Sargents via Oquawka, Pontoosuch, etc., and have filled in the territory encompassed by that trip with red lines. These AIR maps are really wonderful in their accuracy of detail and if you keep checking your points as you go you never get into trouble. The Mississippi magnificent from above. I flew fairly low over it. It was packed with ice and pretty 'formidable' (as the French say it!) The effect of flying as viewed through your own front window and under your own control is quite superior to the effect of viewing the world through the side

windows of a commercial transport. I will be back in
New York soon and we will take some trips together.
We can fly up to the White Mountains in 2 to 3 hours
or to Bear Island, Maine, in 4 hours. I frequently
observed our corona effects and even more frequently
think of you.
As ever,
Dueno B. Fuller

My address in N.Y.C. will be 6 Burns St, Forest Hills.[14]

Naturally Bucky thought Chris would be overjoyed to be
piloted around in the new plane. So when he was in the vicinity
of Lloyds Neck, on Long Island, where Chris had his cabin
called Nostromo, Bucky landed on the water nearby while he
was practising for a seaplane licence. Bucky recalled:

> I flew down to Lloyds Neck and Nostromo and taxied
> up to the swimming place. It was an amphibious plane
> so I could land on water. He was terribly upset, and
> waved at me as if he wanted me to go away. I just
> thought of it as coming home but he let me know he
> thought I was intruding and mustn't come like that
> unannounced. I just thought how lovely it would be![15]

It is possible that Bucky misinterpreted Chris's reaction.
Shortly before this Chris had had to swim out to help two
young people who had got into trouble with their boat among
the underwater rocks just off the shore. He boasted to other
friends about Bucky's having dropped in on him. Unquestionably however, he was becoming more withdrawn and disin-
clined to company unless he himself had arranged the meeting.
He was firmly applying the principle he outlined at Don
Marquis's funeral – energy was not endless – and must be
conserved for one's own work.

Towards the end of 1947 Bucky was back in New York:

December 12, 1947

Dear Christopher:

Are you there?

Am now headquartered at this convenient address – stopped in at Bourkesworks on arrival to see if you were there. They said you had gone to England. I do not use alcohol or other stimulants.

Suggested Xmas Card for people working in Roslyn:

Offending Phonies

Is Euphonious Fun

You Phone Me

And I'll Fo Fum

My telephone No. is

Roslyn 428

The Giant of Green Escape

Another version of this joking comment was retained by Bucky in his Chronofile.[16] Chris's family and friends recognised that his irritability was a symptom of some inner distress and discounted it, but it made them diffident about spur of the moment suggestions.

The Man Who Made Friends with Himself

During the years when Chris was working on his last novel and also on the latest edition of Bartlett, Bucky was beginning to elaborate the theory of the geodesic dome. The plan for a large scale development of the Dymaxion Dwelling Machine had to be abandoned when Beech Aircraft discovered that their commitment to the manufacture of small aircraft for private flying precluded any other changeover in their postwar programme. It was another bitter disappointment for Bucky. He now devoted his time to geometry and structural design. He extended his theories about the Vector Equilibrium and firmly established his own concept of the tetrahedron as a unity of measurement in quantum mechanics. Experimenting with the rigidity which could be achieved by building structures out of interconnecting rods in tetrahedron patterns, he arrived at his combination of three-way, omni-triangulated great circle grids and the geodesic dome.

Helen Hare, who was working on *Bartlett* in Chris's 47th Street office, recalled:

> One vignette is very clear. During the years when designing the geodesic dome was the center of Bucky's life he must have discussed the idea a great deal with Chris. One day (I don't remember the year) Bucky came pounding up the many flights of 46 West 47 Street – Chris's office over the Opportunity Shop. Bucky was

calling out, 'I've got it – I've got it,' and bearing in both hands a roughly put together first model of the dome. At the door he fell breathless over the threshold scattering the small pieces of the model all over the floor. We three spent the rest of the afternoon on our hands and knees collecting the many fragments.[1]

The sponsorship of Bucky's work now came from the academic and architectural world. At Black Mountain College he built early versions of the dome with his students. These were based on the principle of 'Tensegrity' initiated as early as 1927 with a 'Tensegrity' mast. The geodesic dome is derived from a 'Tensegrity' sphere. In November 1948 Bucky wrote to Chris from Chicago on a printed flyer, an offprint from a recent issue of *Science Illustrated*:

BUCKY FULLER'S DYMAXION WORLD
Everybody loves Fuller's incredible houses, automobiles and one-piece bathrooms – but you can't buy them.

++

11/22/48

Dear O.M.
A 22 day in Chicago – Dinner at Riccardo's (All alone as yet on wagon, 1941 . . . to eternity). And many thoughts of you. Am giving seminar to Chi Institute of Design, Oct. 10, '48 to Jan. 31, '49. Advanced classes Architecture and Production Design. Moholy Nagy, its founder died 2 years ago, remember? He too crashed a bed in cocktail party in Congress (Hotel). Love, Bucky[2]

Bucky later kept Chris's reply to his letter inside his copy of *The Man Who Made Friends with Himself*. Both men had reached a peak point in their intellectual achievement and the solitary reaction to it at about the same time. Chris wrote to Bucky:

> *Dec. 14, 1948*
> A happy and imagining Christmas to us all. I finished a few days ago the book I've worked on for four years. Now is the stage of fatigue and reaction and pantheistic poop. But I wanted to be sure you'd stop in at Kroch's store sometime & see yourself p. 996 in the new Bartlett & your coeval Bob Leavitt on p. 999. Next 22 Day, Wed., I'm going to have a Xmas staff luncheon for my faithful adherents at Billy the Oysterman's. I send my dear love & youth to Chicago, Old Loopy. You will like & see meanings in my sombre book but few will. That is their hard luck not ours. Crash a bed or so for me & blessings, O.M.
> Give my love to Mr Kroch.[3]

Bucky's Christmas card for 1948 showed his continuing optimism, in the form of a long poem entitled 'The Historical Attempt by Man to Convert His Evolutions from a Subjective to an Objective Process':

> *In the synchronization of society*
> *towards an objective*
> *evolutionary volition*
> *inspired by deeply acknowledged faith*
> *in an omniscient wisdom and benevolence*
> *instructing through intellect –*
> *(intellect wrote e = mc²) –*
> *intellect may write every equation of*
> *   physical behaviour*
> *but no physical or abstract equation will ever*
> *   compass intellect*
> *or its self starter secret.*

―――――

when the objective evolution
emerges, the intellectually
architectured house of tomorrow
will be central to the emergence.

Bucky wrote on Chris's copy:

Great love to you all
from Allegra, Anne, Bucky[4]

Bucky was very pleased to be quoted in the new *Bartlett* and transferred to the copy he bought at Kroch's the flyleaf from the earlier edition which Chris had given to Bucky and Anne for Christmas in 1937.

During 1948 Chris had concentrated all his extra energy on completing *The Man Who Made Friends with Himself*. Superficially this was a novel about a literary agent, 'authors' representative', as they were beginning to be called. Richard Tolman lived in a suburb and commuted to New York City where he not only had his office but where he was also conducting an affair with his silent partner in the business, a woman psychiatrist, called Zoe. Reading the book casually one might have felt that Chris invented Tolman to represent himself. Wending Ways topographically was very similar to the Roslyn Estates on Long Island, the family home for nearly forty years.

The plot was only a thin veneer. The book was one in which Chris hoped to incorporate symbolically the summation of a lifetime of self-searching philosophy. Few readers understood it when they read it over the first time. Indeed Chris scarcely expected them to do so, as he implied in his comment to Bucky.

Chris probably hoped that his readers would take the trouble to study the book carefully. The importance Bucky attached to the statement that 'Unity is plural and at minimum two' was one key to the symbolism. Bucky applied the statement geometrically but Chris was thinking psychologically. The locus of his thought was Wending Ways, a suburban estate which paralleled in its contours the lobes of the brain.

The main character, Richard Tolman, was Toulemonde, Everyman. He was comic, vulgar, almost pathetic in his struggle to prove his self-importance, but determined to cling to a vision of Truth which he felt could be found in literature, where his predecessors, particularly the poets, had given their answers to the problems of living. In one of the Toulemonde poems written by Chris while he was working on the early stages of the novel, he wrote:

> *The feeling of a day when nothing has*
> *   to be done.*
> *No appointments, absolutely none,*
> *Just to loiter along the shelves*
> *Reintegrating all one's various selves;*
> *And then, when everyone's in bed,*
> *The silence overhead.*
>
> *His blue morocco slippers donned,*
> *What evenings then had Toulemonde.*[5]

The reintegration of Self which Chris attempted in the novel reminds one of the lines in the early poem 'To a Child'

> *Being that now absorbs you all*
> *Harmonious, unit, integral*
> *Will shred into perplexing bits, –*
> *Oh, contradiction of the wits!*[6]

In the novel Chris was reassembling the perplexing bits of his hero's personality. Bucky felt that Chris was continuing in this novel the 'innate exploration of each sense' he first mentioned in 'To a Child'.

Tolman kept a journal for his psychiatrist partner and mistress, Zoe, in order to show her that he could notice and appreciate aspects of life that great minds had seen before him. Zoe's name meant Life. Tolman referred to her as his Life Force. Zoe was also another name for Eve. In the Toulemonde poem which Chris sent to Bucky in 1944 there were a number of lines which revealed that he was thinking of Eve in modern terms:

> *Yes, loved, and lost, and loved some more*
> *And pray there still is love in store*
> *(Short- circuiting Eve's primal curse*
> *By Cupid's lend-lease in reverse) –*
> *Why not drink to Eve, God Bless her,*
> *Before our teeth go on the dresser:*
> *Eve whose praise we have established*
> *In verses prudently unpublished,*
> *Eve with cramps, or Eve at prayers,*
> *Eve no matter what she wears*
> *From bobby socks to Bali bra,*
> *From puberty to grandmamma*
> *See with eye not too serene,*
> *The* bas bleu *or the ballerine,*
> *Goddess, matron, nymph and quean.*[7]

Zoe was more than a symbol. She was a real person in the novel. Use of the name could be associated with Byron's poem 'The Maid of Athens', where the refrain was Ζωή μου, σᾶς ἀγαπῶ (My life, I love you!). Chris had recently re-read it and written a comic verse about it in *Spirit Level*, entitled 'Episode in the Arts'. The use of 'Zoe' as the name of the woman to whom Tolman confided his most intimate ideas as if to himself showed that she was intended to represent something other than just the psychiatrist with whom he was carrying on an affair. If Tolman was Everyman, Zoe Else must provide insight into the problems he faced in respect to his soul's journey through life.

Another character was 'That Man', the phantom self whom Tolman kept on meeting. He saw him on the way to the train. Then he became a neighbour called Mr Doppel-ganger [sic]. Later he appeared at night among the birch trees as well as on other occasions in different disguises. Doppel-ganger signified the duality in man's nature and was the other self with whom Tolman communicated when he was not working out his relationship with Zoe. But he appeared and disappeared as a phantom would. The reader was left with the conclusion that Doppelganger was the person that Tolman would have liked to be.

The most important theme in the novel was Chris's feeling that man's whole life, conscious and subconscious, was a preparation for death. Every individual must somehow integrate and dominate his own experience. The Vasty Hall, the title given to the last chapter of the book, came from the poem by Matthew Arnold: 'Requiescat'. In an earlier quotation from this poem Chris changed a pronoun and combined verses with a hiatus:

> My life was turning, turning
> In mazes of heat and sound . . .
> Tonight it doth inherit
> The vasty hall of death.[8]

Chris felt the individual was threatened by the mindless-ness of modern life which moved faster and faster. The reali-sation of the Great Anxiety had begun with Kafka and Rilke. Tolman wonders whether he was like Kafka in *The Burrow*, 'that appalling story; the most dangerous picture ever written of high-mind pressure'.[9]

Frank Morley drew attention to his brother's quotation from George Herbert's poem 'A Wreath', especially lines three and four in the following passage:

A wreathed garland of deserved praise,
Of praise deserved, unto thee I give,
I give to thee, who knowest all my wayes,
My crooked winding wayes, wherein I live,
Wherein I die, not live: for life is straight,
Straight as a line, and ever tends to thee,
To thee, who art more farre above deceit,
Than deceit seems above simplicitie.
Give me simplicitie, that I may live,
So live and like, that I may know thy wayes,
Know them and practise them: then shall I give
For this poore wreath, give thee a crown of praise.[10]

Herbert clearly meant that the 'Winding Wayes' were the devious and interwoven strands of a man's life which he ultimately would present to God. This poem was one of the final poems which the poet sent to Nicholas Ferrar of Little Gidding just before his death.

Chris rarely gave evidence of his religious life except in his writing. The occasion at Ammonoosuc was an exception. The impression of his family and friends was that while he did not support the Church as an institution he never doubted the existence of God. The choice of a poem by George Herbert to point the underlying meaning of his final novel indicated that he was more influenced by the Christian tradition than most people recognised. Highly interesting too is that in his first novel *Parnassus on Wheels*, the bookseller hero, Roger Mifflin, referred to Herbert's poem 'The Pulley' in his journal, stating:

How gallantly, how reverently they [the Elizabethan poets] tackle the problems of life. When God first made man (says George Herbert) he had a 'glass of blessings standing by'. So he pours on man all the blessings in his reservoir: strength, beauty, wisdom, honour, pleasure – and then he refrains from giving him the last of them, which is rest, i.e. contentment. God sees that if man is contented he will never win his way to Him. Let man be restless so that 'If goodness lead him not, yet weariness/May toss him to my breast.'

Some day I shall write a novel on that theme, and call it *The Pulley*. In this tragic restless world there must be some place where at last we can lay our heads and be at rest. Some people call it death. Some call it God.[11]

The Man Who Made Friends with Himself could have been the novel Chris first thought of thirty years before.

13

'Too Bright for Our Eyes'

After completing *The Man Who Made Friends with Himself* Chris did not attempt another major work. He toyed with the idea of a sequel to *John Mistletoe* but not seriously. He had done what he had set out to do and was content thereafter with collections of poems, essays or other miscellaneous small items, particularly in connection with the Baker Street Irregulars. He also continued broadcasting for the BBC on *Transatlantic Quiz*.

Now that Bucky had achieved the basic design for the dome, which 'harmonised with Nature's own balance of forces in the Universe', the next stage was one of proving the truth of his architectural principle. In 1950 he sent Chris a birthday postcard from Ammonoosuc:

May 5, 1950

Hi Grand Oosuc:–
En route top Mt. Washington to install test structure. Back Forest Hills, N.Y. next week for a few days. (6 Burns Street. Boulevard 8-2639).
B.F.

This was almost immediately followed by a letter:

May 22, 1950

Dear O.M.:–
Since returning from Mt. Wash (where we did pitch

our nylon hemisphere in snow cap and 80 mph wind as test for Arctic Inst) via Maine-N.H. Vermont – have hesitated to telephone due to my hyper-sensitivity to your phonophobia – you may recall my IN DOUBT DON'T rule – at any rate it is a beautiful May 22 day. So here is the love and gladness I would otherwise have tele-electroned to you – Anne had the clipping about dear old Bill Benet. If I were not on wagon we would owe him a very special Rothman evening. I can hear him chortling at the idea. – B.F.[1]

Rothmans was the restaurant where Don Marquis's friends had gathered after his funeral; the first occasion when after the death of a particularly close friend he was commemorated by a gathering of intimates for a drink and a chance to talk about him. Bucky kept the reply he received in his copy of *The Ironing Board*:

> *May 23, Roslyn Heights*
> Dear Old Buckling, It was bonny of you to send me that card of Ammonoosuc. I am truly grateful to you for not having phoned. I have just today got off a job of copy on which I've worked night & day for 3 months with the most appalling interruptions by illness, virus, visit of grandchildren, Uncle FVM being here, grand, but we were both taken pooped. He is living in England again, & nervous prostration of the old dog in her 16th year has nightmares – just when I am snatching a few minutes repose. Bill Benet's death was a nasty shock. The Mt. Washing sounds wonderful. Me writing verse & God bless & love as always old boy, CHRIS
> Bet you didn't notice, you the hero of one of the essays in my book last November.[2]

One of the essays in *The Ironing Board* is entitled 'The Atom Splitter'. This was a name that Chris associated with Bucky so he was probably referring to this. The essay was written about Walt Whitman. Over the years Chris gave Bucky most of his published works. Towards the end of his life he gave Bucky books on the occasion of visits to Roslyn. Bucky received two copies of *Spirit Level*, one dated 13 March 1949 and the other 8 August 1954. He also had a reprint of Chris's tribute to Don Marquis, dated 18 February 1952. This was a copy of Chris's talk at Don's funeral in 1937.

Spirit Level contained a poem stimulated by President Truman's speech in October 1945, known as the Sheep Meadow speech because it was delivered in the Sheep Meadow of Central Park. Before President Truman delivered the speech, Chris had written in *The Commonweal* a version of what he hoped the President might say in addressing himself to 'Fellow Citizens of the World'. He put his feelings more succinctly in a poem:

> *The artist who dreams beauty looks at it*
> *To see what circumstance corroborates;*
> *There is another atom to be split –*
> *The fatal rivalry of sovereign states,*
> *So brace your minds, good sheep, and be fanatics,*
> *The speed of thought arrives, if Einstein's right*
> *As swift as poetry or mathematics –*
> *The square of the velocity of light.*[3]

In 1951 Chris had a stroke. He made a remarkable recovery though his right hand and right side were affected. He was still able to write enough poems to complete a final small collection entitled *Gentlemen's Relish* (1955). His spirit was shown in a lively letter to Bucky's aunt in 1952, a reply to one she had written:

Sunday evg, June 8

Dear Aunt Louise, sweetheart:–

I wish I cd answer yr note as deserves! I was serious ill a yr ago, left me with a semi-palsied right hand; so typing slow & clumsy, handwriting almost illeg. But I must tell you how pleased by yr kind jet-rocket! I hope you may have happened to see today's N.Y. Times Bk Review section wh contains a little piece that might please you – that Scrap Book of yrs sounds like fun, tell me about some of the things in it. I'm struggling, oh so slowly, with another sort of Mistletoe book. Such halcyon days as today's weather sting me a bit in my secret irreparables (spelling?) they move Oh so fast, and as our blessed Chaucer said, my heart was always <u>sliding of corage</u>, viz slippery or skiddery in geist. there is no way to translate Chaucer but by that little inward pain. I hope you have re-read Don Marquis, he truly lived in the street of the White Horse. Oh wonderful Chartres. I bet you never saw my descry (reprinted in *Off the Deep End* or was it *Romany Stain*) of swinging on the bells aloft in the spire! An aweful experience. Helen and I are about to have our 5th grandchild (next month). I'm mostly writing small-wares, zum Beispiel sonnets; the most perfect form of toothache known to man. A sonnet is as excitable to me as a spiral logarithm to the poet Bucky.

Our loves to you all. We shall learn ourselves to keep on learning.

Yr very affte
Christopher[4]

Bucky never lost touch with Chris and continued to send post-cards to ensure that Chris knew he was thinking of him:

June 25, 1952
Here we go across the Mississippi once more (now approaching 100x this time) and for the first time with Anne on our way to speak at Walter Paepcke's Aspen Colorado Conference. MUCH LOVE AND MANY HALOS. Bucky

Nauvou, Ill.

Nauvou House as it Appears Today En Route Wash Unit, St. Louis
Hi! O.M.
They have done a lot of building here since 1939 and turned it into a State Park in 1953. Much love, Bucky

Oct 25, 1954 Minneapolis
Here we go again on way from Univ Michigan to Univ Minnesota, thence Univ No Dakota thence Manitoba, Washington Univ at St. Louis and home for Xmas, All love, Bucky[5]

After his return from England in 1953 Chris discovered that in his absence the Knothole had been broken into and vandalised. All his carefully filed manuscripts and papers and the books on his shelves had been thrown into the middle of the room. It was thought to have been the work of juvenile delinquents – nothing had gone except a small model engine which Chris kept on one of his bookshelves as a memento. The trauma of seeing a life's intellectual work treated in this unfeeling way was more than Chris could bear. A further stroke now greatly reduced his activities. He never went into the Knothole again, nor would he allow anyone else to sort his papers. Ultimately it was done after his death. The collection is now at the University of Texas Harry Ransom Humanities Research

Center. In July 1955 he had a further stroke after which he required round-the-clock nursing care and remained bedridden for the rest of his life.

When Bucky heard how ill Chris was he was hesitant about visiting. Then, by chance, Helen Morley Woodruff, one of Chris's daughters, was driving one day near Huntington, Long Island, with her six-year-old son, Joch, and saw on the horizon a structure which could only be one of Bucky's domes: 'a beautiful ball of sun in the distance'. She drove straight to the site and went in search of Bucky. It was the first time any member of the Morley family had seen one of Bucky's domes. The most successful phase of his career was beginning as Chris's drew to an end.

Bucky recalled:

> It was thanks to young Helen that I realised that Chris would like me to visit him. I went over soon after that. He was upstairs in the room Christopher Junior used to have. He reached out his good arm and hugged me to him. 'Oh Buckling' was what he said. I knew everything was all right between us always.[6]

Some time after this Bucky sent Chris a few lines of verse, written on a lace doily at a restaurant:

TO THE O.M. 10/17/55

AN ICHOATE INTUIT
INTO A COTUIT
THE WORLD IS NAY OYSTER
TO HALF SHELL
OR
STEW IT!   Bucky[7]

This was the final letter in their correspondence. Chris was ill for a very long time. He died on 28 March 1957. Shortly afterwards Bucky wrote to Helen [wife, not daughter]:

> During one of our golden journeys Christopher brought me to my first crossing of the Mississippi as he time and again brought countless friends to their crossings into broader and richer horizons. As at dusk last night I again drove into that now frequently retravelled and beautiful Mississippi country and went over the bridge at Hannibal, my thoughts were all of Christopher. Then west of the river the world-crowned word came that he had now crossed into his great blue beginnings.
>
> Bucky Fuller[8]

One has to remind oneself that the important conversations between Chris and Bucky took place more than fifty years ago. They are still timely now. The influence which Bucky so freely acknowledged that Chris had had on his thinking contributed not merely to *Synergetic Geometry*[9] and the Map but also to the Geodesic Dome. The feeling both men had about coincidence was reinforced when sheer chance led to one of Bucky's domes being built on the line of the 90th meridian. Coincidences occurred over and over again in the course of their friendship culminating in the final one, when Bucky switched on the radio to hear about Chris's death as he was crossing the Mississippi.

Both men would be enormously excited now about the discovery of a carbon molecule with an atomic structure similar to that of a geodesic dome. The coincidence that it should have been carbon, pure household soot we are told, might not have been as surprising to Bucky as to the rest of us. Hugh Kenner in his book *Bucky*, published in 1973, records Bucky's awareness that all known carbon molecules at that time had a tetrahedral structure.[10]

Bucky and Chris did not necessarily agree with each other.

Among Bucky's ideas was the thought that mankind could use the electro-magnetism which he and Chris called 'corona effects' as a means to develop global democracy. Bucky felt that the electro-magnetic energy generated by the human brain could somehow be harnessed to express a positive or a negative response to a proposition which could be put across to the entire human race simultaneously. This would involve a super-power which had at its disposal the sort of electronic devices which so far have been used for surveillance by satellite.[11]

Chris, however, did not fully agree with Bucky's views about comprehensive planning. Who would control the super-power? Chris felt that this kind of solution would not be possible until 'men about town' became 'men about planet'. Freedom of speech was freedom to exercise judgement. The power to exercise it for oneself should not be delegated. To Chris the problem of mind erosion and the possibility that the human race could lose its capacity to think for itself as technological progress escalated was a serious one.

From their discussion of the cosmic religious sense came the thought that there may be different aspects of reality into which we are tuned at any one time. They found the theories of J.W. Dunne a possible confirmation of their own views on pre-cognitive dreams and a moving time dimension.

Bucky felt that he and Chris throughout their lives had been trying to say the same thing each in a different way. Essentially the universe is a continuing tendency towards 'one-ness' and as it gets nearer and nearer so it gets close to perfection. Since it never achieves one-ness, 'Unity is plural and at minimum two', but the universe is operating four dimensionally. As Bucky put it:

> Faith in the intellectual integrity of great scientific laws which can only be expressed mathematically provides absolute proof that a greater intellect than man's is operating in the universe. Mathematics is purely intel-

lectual so these great laws are inherently intellectual. None are found to contradict others. This manifest intellectual integrity I call God.[12]

This comment of Bucky's was certainly very close indeed to the one made by Chris in *Where the Blue Begins*:

It begins to look as though life might be a kind of locus whose commanding equation we call God.[13]

Bucky thought that not only was Chris ahead of his time but he sacrificed the chance to be one of the great minds of the century by 'just the elfin in him. He couldn't take himself seriously.' His ideas were beginning now to come into phase. Chris in fact foresaw his own future when he stated that the scientist sometimes succeeds but the poet never does. He fulfilled his own purpose and that is what matters. His comment that the only success is to be able to live your life in your own way continues to be quoted on greeting cards.[14]

To both Bucky and Chris a sense of significance was the divine spark which, once ignited, illuminated understanding. They fired one another's enthusiasms. The interaction of their ideas operated synergetically in the evolution of a philosophy of self and universe, man and society. Chris called Bucky 'The Atom Splitter' and elsewhere remarked that the atom which remained for man to split was the fatal rivalry of sovereign states. It still is. He did what he could in his lifetime to draw attention to Truth and Beauty as handed on to us from a great literary past and as the source from which contemporary man could draw the wisdom he would require. Only in understanding himself in relation to others could man contribute to the accomplishment of the divine purpose and combat the forces which seek to destroy rather than to create. For Bucky the geodesic dome was more than a structure. It was as symbol of Earth's unity. Earth's unity is the destiny 'too bright for our eyes'.

Christopher Morley Chronology

1890. Christopher Darlington Morley is born on 5 May, the eldest of three sons, to Lillian Bird Morley and Frank Morley in Haverford, Pennsylvania.

1900. The family moves to Baltimore, where Frank Morley, a noted mathematician, teaches at Johns Hopkins University.

1906–1910. Attends Haverford College; edits school literary magazine and is elected to Phi Beta Kappa.

1910–1913. Studies modern history at New College, Oxford, as a Rhodes Scholar.

1912. Publishes in England *The Eighth Sin*, his first volume of poetry.

1913–1917. Works for Doubleday, Page and Company at Garden City, New York, learning every aspect of the book trade.

1914. Marries Helen Booth Fairchild; they later have four children, Christopher Jr, Louise, Helen and Blythe.

1917–1920. Lives in Philadelphia, first as an editor of the *Ladies' Home Journal*, then as columnist for the *Philadelphia Evening Public Ledger*.

1918. Publishes *Shandygaff*, the first of thirteen collections of essays.

1920. Begins life-long residence at 'Green Escape', Roslyn, Long Island, New York.

1920–1923. Writes 'The Bowling Green' column in the *New York Evening Post*.

1922. Publishes *Where the Blue Begins*; edits *Modern Essays*, a popular anthology for schools.

1924–1944. Acts as contributing editor of the *Saturday Review of Literature*, responsible for 'The Bowling Green' column for fourteen years, and the 'Trade Winds' column for fifteen.

1925. Publishes *Thunder on the Left*.

1926–1954. Serves as judge of the Book-of-the-Month Club.

1927. Doubleday publishes twelve-volume *Haverford Collected Edition* of Morley's works.

1928–1930. Presents popular series of old melodramas at two theatres in Hoboken, New Jersey.

1931. Publishes the autobiographical *John Mistletoe*; lectures at the University of Pennsylvania (published as *Ex Libris Carissimis*).

1932. Publishes *Human Being*.

1933. Founds the Baker Street Irregulars.

1937. Edits the eleventh edition of Bartlett's *Familiar Quotations* with the assistance of Louella Everett.

1938. Publishes *History of an Autumn*, long essay on events at Munich.

1939. Publishes *Kitty Foyle*, his best-selling novel.

1942. Publishes *Thorofare*.

1948. Publishes revised twelfth edition of *Bartlett's Familiar Quotations*.

1949. Publishes *The Man Who Made Friends with Himself*, his last novel.

1951. Suffers the first of three incapacitating strokes.

1955. Publishes *Gentlemen's Relish*, his last volume of poems.

1957. Morley dies, 28 March.

Source: Mark Wallach and Jon Bracker, *Christopher Morley*, G.K. Hall & Co., 1976, with minor amendments.

Richard Buckminster Fuller Chronology

Editors' note: As Louise pointed out, Bucky's career began to take off as Chris's reached its peak. The full details of Bucky's inventions, designs, architectural projects, and associated writing and lecturing can be found in the timeline at the Buckminster Fuller Institute website: https://bfi.org/. The chronology below is limited to the period covered in this book: 1895–1957. Bucky died on 12 July 1983. In 1983 he was awarded the Presidential Medal of Freedom, the country's highest civilian honour, by President Ronald Reagan.

1895. Richard Buckminster Fuller is born in Milton, Massachusetts, 12 July, second of four children of Richard Buckminster and Caroline Wolcott (Andrews).

1904–1913. Attends Milton Academy, Massachusetts.

1913. Attends Milton Academy, Massachusetts.

1913. Studies at Harvard University.

1914–1915. Works as apprentice machine fitter, Richards, Atkinson, & Haserick, Boston, importers of cotton mill machinery.

1915. Resumes studies at Harvard University.

1915–1917. Works in various apprentice jobs, Armour & Co, New York City.

1917. Attends US Naval Academy, Annapolis, Maryland. Marries Anne Hewlett on 12 July, at Rock Hall, Lawrence, Long Island, New York. They later have two children: Alexandra Willets (1918–1922); Allegra (Fuller Snyder), born 1927.

1917–1919. Serves in United States Navy, World War I: Ensign USNR to Lieutenant USN.

1919–1921. Works as Assistant Export Manager, Armour & Company.

1922. Works as National Account Sales Manager, Kelly – Springfield Truck Company.

1922–1927. President, Stockade Building Systems.

1930–1932. Editor and Publisher, *Shelter* magazine. Assistant to Director of Research, Pierce Foundation & American Radiator Standard Manufacturing Company; produces mass-production kitchen and bathroom back to back.

1932–1936. Director and Chief Engineer, Dymaxion Corporation, Bridgeport, Connecticut; produces three Dymaxion cars.

1936–1938. Assistant to Director, Research and Development, Phelps Dodge Corporation.

1937. Designs Dymaxion bathroom prototypes (twelve made). One installed in the Knothole.

1938–1940. Science and Technology Consultant, *Fortune* magazine.

1938. Publishes *Nine Chains to the Moon*.

1940–1942. Vice President, Chief Engineer, Dymaxion Company, Inc., Delaware; also associated with Butler Manufacturing Company. Produces Dymaxion Dwelling Unit (DDU).

1942–1944. Serves as Chief Mechanical Engineer, US Board of Economic Warfare, World War II. Special Assistant to Deputy Director, US Foreign Economic Administration.

1943. Dymaxion Map is published in *LIFE* magazine.

1944–1946. Chairman of Board, Chief Engineer, Dymaxion Dwelling Machine Corporation (later Fuller Houses), Beech Aircraft Company, Wichita, Kansas.

1946. Receives patent for the Dymaxion Map.

1947–1949. Professor at Black Mountain College, North Carolina, for three summer sessions.

1948. Starts to teach at Massachusetts Institute of Technology (MIT). Works on prototype geodesic structures.

1950. Begins extensive programme of public lectures worldwide, which continue until his death in 1983.

1953. Completes first practical application of a geodesic dome, for Ford Motor Company's River Rouge Headquarters.

1954. Receives patent for the geodesic dome.

1955. Installation of geodesic radome in the Arctic.

1956. Is appointed visiting lecturer at Southern Illinois University.

Sources: Chronofile in *The Buckminster Fuller Reader* (ed. James Meller, London: Jonathan Cape, 1970); Lloyd Steven Sieden, *Buckminster Fuller's Universe* (Perseus Publishing: Cambridge, Mass., 1989); the timeline on the Buckminster Fuller Institute website (https://bfi.org/).

Notes

Preface
1 Editors' Note: The Center has been renamed the Harry Ransom Center but we have left Louise's references to 'HRHRC' unchanged.

Chapter 1
1 Christopher Morley, 'The Sense of Significance', *The Romany Stain*, Garden City, NY, Doubleday, Page & Company, 1926, p. 48; also source for Chris's 'Confirmation' quotation, on p. 2 (p. 160).
2 Buckminster Fuller, Letter to LC, 19-7-76.
3 Christopher Morley, *Inward Ho!*, Garden City, NY, Doubleday, Page & Company, 1923, p. 105.
4 Christopher Morley, 'To a Child', *Chimneysmoke*, New York, George H. Doran Company, 1921.
5 RBF/LC Interview, 5-11-75 (C1115/02).
6 Buckminster Fuller, *Nine Chains to the Moon*, Philadelphia, PA, J.B. Lippincott Company, 1938; quotation *Saturday Review of Literature* Fortieth Anniversary edition, 1962; Interview RBF/LC 17-11-75 (C1115/03).
7 Buckminster Fuller, Letter to Christopher Morley, 1928, republished in *4D Timelock*, Carbondale, IL, R. B. Fuller, 1972, p. 46.
8 Christopher Morley, *I Know a Secret*, Garden City, NY, Doubleday, Page & Company, 1927, pp. 166–168.
9 RBF/LC Interview, 29-6-76 (C1115/10).
10 RBF/LC Interviews, 23–25-3-1976 (C1115/07/08/09).
11 Christopher Morley, *Thunder on the Left*, Garden City, NY, Doubleday, Page & Company, 1925, pp. 139, 143, 149.
12 Christopher Morley, *Human Being*, Garden City, NY, Doubleday, Doran & Company, 1931; London, Faber & Faber, 1933, p. 150.
13 RBF/LC Interview, 23-3-76 (C1115/07).
14 Christopher Morley, 'Coldest and Hottest', *Christopher Morley's Briefcase*, Philadelphia, PA, J.B. Lippincott Company, 1936, p. 17.

Chapter 2

1 RBF/LC Interviews, 23-9-75 (C1115/01); 17-11-75 (C1115/04).
2 Christopher Morley, in column entitled 'Bowling Green', *Saturday Review of Literature*, republished, Christopher Morley, *Streamlines*, Garden City, NY, Doubleday, Doran & Company, 1936, Faber & Faber, 1937, p. 32.
3 Buckminster Fuller Chronofile, Stanford University, CA (hereafter Chronofile).
4 Christopher Morley Correspondence, Harry Ransom Humanities Research Center, University of Texas, Austin, TX (hereafter HRHRC).
5 RBF/LC Interviews, 17-11-75 (C1115/03); 29-6-76 (C1115/11).
6 '22 Days' discussed RBF/LC Interviews 23-9-75 (C1115/01); 30-6-76 (C1115/12).
7 See back of CM Diary, 19 July 1938, No. 47, HRHRC.
8 *Saturday Review of Literature*, undated clipping retained by RBF in Chronofile.
9 'New moon feeling' discussed RBF/LC Interview 30-6-76 (C1115/12). *Translations from the Chinese*, New York, George H. Doran Company, 1922.
10 Christopher Morley, *Where the Blue Begins*, Garden City, NY, Doubleday, Page & Co, 1922, p. 21.
11 RBF/LC Interview, 23-3-76 (C1115/07).
12 Christopher Morley, 'Principality and Power', Presentation book for World's Fair, New York City, 1936.
13 RBF/LC Interview, 24-3-76 (C1115/08).
14 Discussions of Professor Frank Morley's theorem and influence of mathematical ideas, RBF/LC Interviews, 17-11-75 (C1115/03); 24-3-76 (C1115/08). See also Louise Cochrane, 'Camaraderie & Coincidence', *Haverford* (Alumni Magazine) Fall 1992.

Chapter 3

1 Christopher Morley, 'Dedication', *Streamlines*, Garden City, NY, Doubleday, Doran & Company, 1936, London, Faber & Faber, 1937.
2 Christopher Morley, *Inward Ho!*, Garden City, NY, Doubleday, Page & Company, 1923, pp. 113, 110–111.
3 Christopher Morley, *The Romany Stain*, Garden City, NY, Doubleday, Page & Company, 1926, p. 227.
4 Christopher Morley, *John Mistletoe*, Garden City, NY, Doubleday, Doran & Company, 1931, p. 337, 339.
5 Christopher Morley, *John Mistletoe*, p. 347.
6 Letter from Keats to Reynolds quoted by Norman Cousins, *Saturday Review of Literature*, 20 April 1957.
7 RBF/LC Interviews, 24-3-76 (C1115/08); 29-6-76 (C1115/11).

8 Christopher Morley, 'Streamlines (Thoughts in a Dymaxion Car)', *Streamlines*, p. 32. [Editors' Note: text adjusted slightly for clarity.]

9 'Thoughts in a Dymaxion Car', p. 33.

10 Christopher Morley, 'Epistle to the Colossians', *Streamlines*, pp. 75, 77.

11 Christopher Morley, 'Mind Erosion', *Streamlines*, p. 50.

12 Christopher Morley, 'Mind Erosion', p. 47.

13 Isamu Noguchi, *The Sculptor's World*, New York, Thames & Hudson, 1967, pp. 23, 24, Plates 30–33. The telegram is quoted in R. Buckminster Fuller, *Nine Chains to the Moon*, pp. 62–63.

14 Christopher Morley, 'Mind Erosion', p. 52.

15 RBF/LC Interview, 24-3-76 (C1115/08).

Chapter 4

1 Flyer sent to RBF in Chronofile, 1937.

2 RBF/LC Interview, 29-6-76 (C1115/10).

3 RBF/LC Interview, 24-3-76 (C1115/08).

4 R. Buckminster Fuller, *An Autobiographical Monologue/Scenario*, documented and edited by Robert Snyder, New York, St Martin's Press, 1970, pp. 68–70.

5 RBF/LC Interviews, 23-9-75 (C1115/01); 17-11-75 (C1115/03); 23, 24-3-76 (C1115/ 07/08).

6 Christopher Morley, 'Principality and Power', New York World's Fair, 1936.

7 RBF/LC Interview, 23-3-76 (C1115/07).

8 Christopher Morley, *John Mistletoe*, pp. 226–227.

9 RBF/LC Interview, 17-11-75 (C1115/03).

10 RBF/LC Interviews, 23-9-75 (C1115/01); 25-3-76 (C1115/09).

11 RBF/LC Interviews, 23-9-75 (C1115/01); 29-6-76 (C1115/10).

12 Christopher Morley, 'Preface', *Bartlett's Familiar Quotations* (eleventh edition), ed. Christopher Morley, Boston, MA, Little Brown, 1933, republished in Christopher Morley, *Prefaces without Books*, selected by Herman Abromson, Introduction by Jerome Weidman, Austin, TX, University of Texas, 1970, p. 151.

13 Christopher Morley, 'Tribute to Don Marquis', privately published and circulated after Marquis's death, 1938, Chronofile.

14 RBF/LC Interview, 5-11-75 (C1115/04).

Chapter 5

1 Installation of Dymaxion bathroom in Christopher Morley's Knothole. CM Diary 46, June 1938.

2 Chronofile.

3 RBF/LC Interviews, 25-3-76 (C1115/09); 17-11-75 (C1115/03).

4 CM Diaries, 1938.

5 R. Buckminster Fuller, *Nine Chains to the Moon*, Predictions mentioned in interviews, 23-9-75 (C1115/01); 17-11-75 (C1115 /03). They were not republished in later editions, 1963, 1971.
6 RBF/LC Interviews, 5-11-75 (C1115/02); 29-6-76(C1115/10). See also Christopher Morley, *History of an Autumn*, Philadelphia, PA, and New York, J.B. Lippincott Company, 1938, p. 11.
7 CM Diaries July, August 1938, No. 47 (Back of diary reads in reverse).
8 RBF/LC Interview, 29-6-76 (C1115/11).
9 Christopher Morley, *Where the Blue Begins*, pp. 78, 81.
10 R. Buckminster Fuller, *Nine Chains to the Moon*, p. 134
11 RBF/LC Interview, 17-11-75 (C1115/ 03).
12 Christopher Morley, 'Ammonoosuc', *The Middle Kingdom*, New York, Harcourt Brace & Co. 1944, pp. 8–9.

Chapter 6

1 CM Diary, 1938, Supplementary Notebook, HRHRC (34). [Editors' Note: CM is quoting his own phrase from *The Trojan Horse*, London, Faber and Faber, 1938, spoken by Cressida (p. 243), and the title of Chapter 21.]
2 RBF/LC Interview, 25-3-76 (C1115/09).
3 CM Diary, 1938, HRHRC (34).
4 RBF/LC Interview, 30-6-76 (C1115/12); CM Diary (47).
5 Christopher Morley, 'The Sense of Significance', *Romany Stain*, 1926.
6 CM Diary fragment, HRHRC.
7 CM Diary Supplementary Notebook (42).
8 CM Diary (48).
9 Chronofile.
10 Chronofile.
11 RBF/LC Interviews, 5-11-75 (C1115/02); 29-6-76 (C1115/11); 17-11-75 (C1115/03).
12 Christopher Morley, *History of an Autumn*, quoting from his diary, p. 18.
13 Letter should be in collection at HRHRC (not found). [Editors' Note: The biography of CDM by Mark Wallach and Jon Bracker quotes from Franklin D. Roosevelt's letter of 21 December 1938, which suggests it was in HRHRC when they did their research. See *Christopher Morley*, Boston, MA, G.K. Hall & Co., 1976, p. 42.]
14 CM Diary, January 1939 (51).
15 Chronofile.
16 RBF/LC Interview, 22-11-75 (C1115/06).
17 Chronofile.
18 Chronofile.

Chapter 7

1 Chronofile.
2 Diary 51, 1939.
3 Diary 51, 1939.
4 Diary 51, 1939.
5 Christopher Morley, *Kitty Foyle*, Philadelphia, PA, J.B. Lippincott Company, 1939, pp. 65–66, 338.
6 Diary 51, 1939 (53).
7 Diary 51, 1939 (71, 72, 73).
8 Diary 52, 1939 (4).
9 Chronofile.
10 RBF/LC Interviews, 5-11-75 (C1115/02); 24-3-76 (C1115/08); 29-6-76 (C1115/10).
11 RBF/LC Interview, 17-11-75 (C1115/03).
12 Diary 53, Nov. 1940.
13 RBF/LC Interviews, 5-11-75 (C1115 02); 23-3-76 (C1115/07); 17-11-75 (C1115/03).
14 RBF/LC Interview, 23-3-76 (C1115/07). Letter, Chronofile, Carbon, HRHRC.
15 CM Collection HRHRC.
16 Chronofile.
17 HRHRC – date presumably 1941 when the structure was tested.
18 HRHRC.
19 Chronofile.

Chapter 8

1 Christopher Morley, 'Tempest 1941', *Saturday Review of Literature*, April 1941, republished as *The Ironing Board*, Garden City, NY, Doubleday & Company, 1949; London, Faber and Faber, 1950, pp. 196–208.
2 Book-of-the-Month Club News, May 1941.
3 RBF Letter to CM, HRHRC.
4 Chronofile.
5 RBF/LC Interviews, 23-9-75 (C1115/01); 5-11-75 (C1115/02); 17-11-75 (C1115/04); 24-3-76 (C1115/08).
6 Chronofile.
7 R. Buckminster Fuller, *No More Secondhand God*, Carbondale, IL, Southern Illinois Press, 1963, p. 28; Christopher Morley, ed., *Bartlett's Familiar Quotations* (12th edition), Boston, MA, Little Brown, 1948.
8 RBF/LC Interview, 24-3-76 (C1115/08).
9 Invitation from Felix Morley conveyed by CM, Chronofile.
10 HRHRC.
11 Chronofile.

12 HRHRC.
13 HRHRC.

Chapter 9

1 HRHRC.
2 Chronofile.
3 Chronofile.
4 HRHRC.
5 Christopher Morley, 'The Spoken Word', December 1942, *The Middle Kingdom*, p. 41.
6 Article on 'Books for the Armed Forces', 1942.
7 HRHRC; RBF/LC Interview 25-3-76.
8 Notes for unpublished novel, *The House of Fame*, HRHRC.
9 RBF/LC Interview, 25-3-76 (C1115/07). Autographed World's Fair Book is in Knothole Collection (Christopher Morley papers), Bryant Library, Roslyn, Long Island, New York. This copy has original drawings by RBF of the development of the Dymaxion theory.
10 RBF/LC Interviews, 17-11-75 (C1115/04); 25-3-76. Correspondence in Chronofile and HRHRC.
11 Chronofile.
12 Chronofile.
13 HRHRC.
14 Chronofile.
15 RBF/LC Interviews, 17-11-75 (C1115/04), 25-3-76 (C1115/09).

Chapter 10

1 HRHRC.
2 HRHRC.
3 Chronofile.
4 RBF/LC Interview, 23-3-76 (C1115/07).
5 HRHRC.
6 RBF/LC Interview, 23-3-76 (C1115/07).
7 HRHRC.
8 RBF/LC Interview, 23-3-76 (C1115/07).
9 Chronofile.
10 HRHRC.
11 *Sherlock Holmes' Prayer*, published by Baker Street Irregulars, New York, 1944.

Chapter 11

1 Chronofile.
2 HRHRC.
3 Chronofile.

4 Christopher Morley, *The Man Who Made Friends with Himself*, Garden City, NY, Doubleday & Company, 1949.
5 HRHRC.
6 Postcards, Buckminster Fuller to Christopher Morley, HRHRC.
7 Chronofile.
8 Christopher Morley, 'Ballad of New York, New York', *The Ballad of New York, New York and Other Poems, 1930–1950*', Garden City, NY, Doubleday & Company, 1950.
9 HRHRC.
10 HRHRC.
11 HRHRC. E.J. Applewhite, *Cosmic Fishing*, New York, Macmillan Publishing Company, 1977, is an account of his later collaboration with Buckminster Fuller on the writing of *Synergetics*.
12 Chronofile.
13 HRHRC.
14 HRHRC.
15 RBF/LC Interview, 17-11-75 (C1115/04).
16 HRHRC and Chronofile.

Chapter 12

1 Letter from Helen Hare Cain to Louise Cochrane, 10 April 1976. For accounts of the development of the dome see Robert Marks, *The Dymaxion World of Buckminster Fuller*, New York, Reinhold Publishing Corporation, 1966, pp. 156 et seq.; Hugh Kenner, *Bucky, A Guided Tour of Buckminster Fuller*, New York, William Morrow & Company, 1973; Hugh Kenner, *Geodesic Math and How to Use it*, Berkeley, Los Angeles, CA, London, University of California Press, 1976.
2 HRHRC.
3 RBF Library (his personal copies of books). Letter kept in *Bartlett's Familiar Quotations*.
4 HRHRC.
5 Christopher Morley, 'Toulemonde Desipient', *The Middle Kingdom*, p. 49.
6 Christopher Morley, 'To a Child', *Chimneysmoke*, New York, George H. Doren Company, 1921.
7 Christopher Morley, 'Toulemonde Intermezzo', *The Middle Kingdom*, pp. 55–58.
8 Henry Newbolt, *The Poems of Matthew Arnold*, London and Edinburgh, Thomas Nelson & Sons Ltd, 'Requiescat', p. 144.
9 *The Man Who Made Friends With Himself*, p. 96. [Editors' Note: passage slightly amended to make clear that that these were Tolman's thoughts.]
10 Frank Morley, in conversation with LC. 'A Wreath', in *The Poems of*

George Herbert, London, Oxford University Press, 1961, p. 176.

11 Christopher Morley, *Parnassus on Wheels*, Garden City, NY, Doubleday, Doran & Company, 1917, republished by Avon Books, New York,
1983, p. 120.

Chapter 13

1 HRHRC.
2 RBF Library, letter in Christopher Morley, *The Ironing Board* (1949).
3 Christopher Morley, 'The Sheep Meadow', *Spirit Level and Other
Poems*, Cambridge, MA, Harvard University Press, 1946, p. 25.
4 Letter preserved by RBF in Chronofile.
5 HRHRC.
6 RBF/LC Interview, 25-3-76 (C1115/09).
7 HRHRC.
8 HRHRC, copy in Chronofile.
9 R. Buckminster Fuller, in collaboration with E.J. Applewhite, *Synergetics,* New York, Macmillan Publishing Co. Inc., 1975.
10 Explained by Hugh Kenner, *Bucky: A Guided Tour of Buckminster
Fuller*, p. 118. See also Robert Marks, *The Dymaxion World of Buckminster Fuller*, pp. 40–48.
11 Hearings before the Committee on Foreign Relations United States
Senate, Ninety-Fourth Congress, Washington, DC, 15 May 1975, 'The
United States and the United Nations', statement by R. Buckminster
Fuller.
12 RBF/LC Interview, 29-6-76 (C1115/10).
13 Christopher Morley, *Where the Blue Begins*, p. 78.
14 Christopher Morley, *Where the Blue Begins*, p. 85.